Reading A Lease Credit
The Phone Book Checks
Guarantees Classified Ads
Taxes Bank Statements

Life Skills Reading

by Carol Mullins

Food Labels Utility Bills
Drug Labels What's on TV
Getting Paid Road Signs
Want Ads The Dictionary
Agreements Paying Bills
Product Labels Tests
Driver's License Reading

Educational Design, Inc., 47 West 13th Street, New York, NY 10011 212 255-7900

Acknowledgements:

Legal forms reprinted with the permission of
and available from Julius Blumberg, Inc.,
New York, New York 10013.

IFE SKILLS READING

Table of Contents

Introduction

Some things you read because you want to. Other things you read because you need to. The things you need to read are Life Skills Reading.

Life Skills Reading is the kind of reading you do almost every day of your life. Reading signs. Labels. Instructions. Looking up things in the phone book. Even reading maps or timetables.

It's the kind of reading you have to do when you fill out forms—when you apply for a job, or for a driver's license, or for credit. It's reading the instructions in a mail-order catalog and filling out the order form correctly so you can get what you want.

It's reading—and understanding—all the pieces of paper in your life that deal with money. Checks. Bills. Bank Statements. Pay Statements. Tax Forms. And many others.

The thirty-six lessons in this book will help you develop your skills at this kind of reading.

Unit I.
READING LABELS

Reading labels is an everyday part of Life Skills Reading.

Clothing labels tell you the sizes that fit you. They tell you how to take care of the clothing so that it stays clean and neat.

Food labels tell you how to store and prepare food. They also tell you what's in the food, so you can plan a healthy diet.

Drug labels tell you how to use medicine. If you don't follow the directions, the medicine may not work. It may even harm you or others in your family.

Product labels tell you how to use a product properly. They also warn you about ways the product may be dangerous or harmful.

CONTENTS OF THIS UNIT

1. Food Labels

READ the label below.
NOTICE what kinds of information are on food labels.
STUDY the WORDS AND MEANINGS.
ANSWER the QUESTIONS.

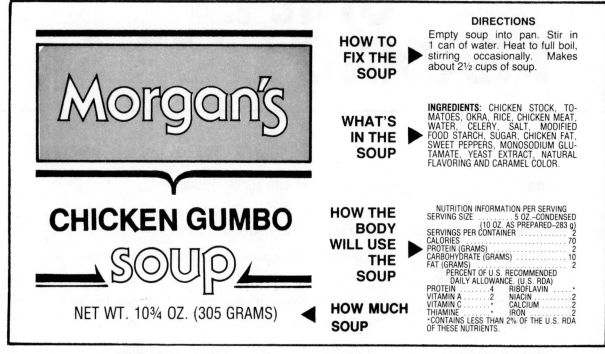

FRONT OF CAN   BACK OF CAN

WORDS AND MEANINGS

ingredients—what a product contains or is made of

perishable—spoils easily

nutrition—the way the body takes in and uses food

calories—units of food energy. When you eat more calories than you need, you gain weight

net wt.—weight of what's inside the package

oz.—ounce

lb.—pound

gram—a weight in the metric system, about the weight of a paper clip

QUESTIONS   Check (✔) the box next to the correct answer.

1. What must you add before you heat the soup?

☐ 1 can of milk
☐ 1 can of water
☐ nothing

2. Net wt. is the weight of

☐ can plus food
☐ food only

3. Tomatoes make Ethan sick. Read the list of ingredients in the soup above. Can Ethan eat this soup?

☐ yes   ☐ no

4. Marge wants to keep down the number of calories she eats. Which is better for her?

☐ 1/2 cup of peas, about 30 calories
☐ a serving of Morgan's Chicken Gumbo (Find the calories under Nutrition Information and compare)

5. How many ounces of soup are in the can on the last page?

_____ounces

6. **UNIT PRICE LABELS** are sometimes on shelves under the food. They help you compare prices. Look at the unit price labels at the right. For 1 pound of soup, which brand costs less?

☐ Atlas ☐ Morgan's

COMPARE PRICES FOR 1 POUND OF SOUP

UNIT PRICE	YOU PAY		UNIT PRICE	YOU PAY
54.2¢ PER POUND	**34¢**		**52.1¢** PER POUND	**35¢**
ATLAS SOUP			MORGAN'S SOUP	

7. Which orange drink has more orange juice in it?

☐ Elmo's ☐ Sunny's

ELMO'S ORANGE DRINK 2% ORANGE JUICE

SUNNY'S ORANGE DRINK 10% ORANGE JUICE

8. Sometimes milk is stamped with a date. The store shouldn't sell the milk after that date. The later the date, the fresher the milk. Which milk do you think is fresher?

☐ Dec. 14 ☐ Dec. 17

DEC. 14   DEC. 17

MILK   MILK

½ PINT   ½ PINT

9. This chicken pie thawed when the electricity went off. Now the electricity is fixed. What should you do with the pie?

☐ eat it tonight for dinner
☐ put it back in the freezer

CHICKEN PIE

DO NOT REFREEZE

10. What can't you do with this fish?

☐ cook it right away
☐ leave it on the table overnight
☐ put it in the refrigerator

FISH

PERISHABLE

L.5 LB.

2. Clothing Labels

READ the shirt label below.

NOTICE what kinds of information are on clothes labels.

STUDY the WORDS AND MEANINGS.

ANSWER the QUESTIONS on the next page.

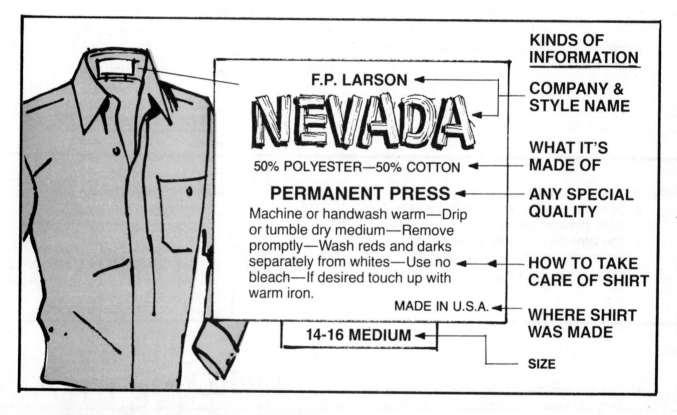

WORDS AND MEANINGS

polyester

nylon

Dacron® — Types of cloth that are washable, need little or no ironing, and usually don't shrink. (Dacron® is a trade name for Dupont's polyester.)

cotton—cloth that needs ironing and will shrink when washed—unless it's mixed with polyester, nylon or Dacron. Preshrunk or Sanforized cotton will still need ironing, but it won't shrink much.

Sanforized®—cotton cloth treated so it will shrink very little.

preshrunk—cotton cloth that will shrink a little more than Sanforized® but still not very much.

colorfast—color will not come out in the wash.

permanent press—needs little or no ironing. The problem is that if you let out a hem, you can never iron out the old crease.

waterproof—water will not go through. Air won't either, so you may feel hot and sticky wearing it.

water-repellent—most water will slide off, but not all.

QUESTIONS

1. The shirt on the last page is red. Can you wash it with your white sheets?

☐ yes   ☐ no

2. COLORFAST is on the label of another red shirt. If you wash it with your white sheets, will they turn pink?

☐ yes   ☐ no

---

3. Which pair of pants is more likely to need ironing?

☐ 1   ☐ 2

4. Which pair of pants will probably look worse if you let them out at the bottom?

☐ 1   ☐ 2

1 —
Sandy Sawyer
100% COTTON • PRESHRUNK
MACHINE WASHABLE
MADE IN USA

2 —
A.L.Lowe's WORK CLOTHES
50% COTTON • 50% POLYESTER
PERMANENT PRESS
MACHINE WASH/TUMBLE DRY LOW
MADE IN USA

---

5. Which jacket will keep water out even in a heavy storm?

☐ 1   ☐ 2

6. How can you clean Jacket 1?

☐ at the dry cleaners
☐ in a washing machine
☐ by hand

1 —
MADE IN TAIWAN
WATERPROOF 65% PVC 35% NYLON
WIPE CLEAN WITH DAMP CLOTH
• DO NOT DRY CLEAN
• DO NOT MACHINE WASH   **M**

2 —
Paris MADE IN FRANCE
• 100% DACRON
• WATER REPELLENT
• MACHINE WASH
• NO CHLORINE BLEACH

---

7. Which shirt will probably shrink the most?
☐ 1   ☐ 2   ☐ 3

8. Which shirt will probably shrink the least?
☐ 1   ☐ 2   ☐ 3

9. Which shirt is largest?
☐ 1   ☐ 2   ☐ 3

10. Which shirt was made in America?
☐ 1   ☐ 2   ☐ 3

1 —
Best's & Co.   32-34 MED
• **100% COTTON**
• **SANFORIZED®** MADE IN USA

2 —
MADE IN INDIA   **naga**   36-38 LARGE
100% COTTON
HAND WASH SEPARATELY

3 —
SUPER FIT
100% COTTON
PRESHRUNK
MADE IN ITALY
SMALL 8-10

3. Product Labels

LOOK at the detergent box below.

FIND the following kinds of information:

1. HOW TO OPEN IT
2. WHAT IT'S GOOD FOR
3. DIRECTIONS FOR USE
4. CAUTIONS (what to be careful of)
5. BRAND NAME
6. WEIGHT OF CONTENTS

LAUNDRY DETERGENT

Wish

DETERGENT

CAUTION
EYE IRRITANT

NET WT. 20 OZ

FRONT

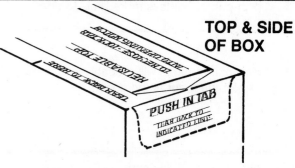

TOP & SIDE OF BOX

PUSH IN TAB

USAGE INSTRUCTIONS:

To get the best cleaning results with Wish, a proper concentration of Wish in the wash water is required. The amount of Wish to use will vary with washing conditions. For example, in cooler or harder water or with heavily soiled or large loads, you will probably want to use more Wish. In softer water or with lightly soiled or smaller loads, you can probably use less Wish. Remember, ALWAYS MEASURE the amount of Wish you need for each load.

TOP-LOADING AUTOMATICS [1] [¼] Normal Capacity—Start with 1¼ cups of Wish.

FRONT-LOADING AUTOMATICS
Start with ½ **cup** of Wish or enough to bring suds ⅓ to ½ way up the window.

WRINGER WASHERS Start with **1 1/2 cups** of Wish.

FROM BACK OF BOX

WORDS AND MEANINGS

incinerate—burn

discard—throw away

physician—doctor

irritant—something that burns or hurts the skin or eyes

absorb—take in or soak up

inhale—breathe in

ventilation—way to bring in fresh air

internally—inside the body

poison ☠ —can **KILL**

QUESTIONS

1. Wish detergent may hurt your
   ☐ eyes ☐ skin

2. How much Wish goes into each of these washing machines? Write your answer above each picture.

3. Sani-Sink fixes stopped up sinks. The label says **POISON** ☠ . Which should you be more careful with?
   ☐ Sani-Sink ☐ Wish

___ CUPS ___ CUPS ___ CUPS

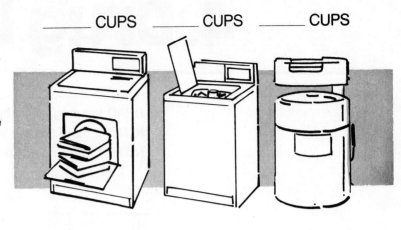

4. To get the top off this can:
   ☐ squeeze, pull, and twist
   ☐ turn left and unscrew

5. This spray is not good for:
   ☐ ants ☐ flies ☐ roaches

6. The Cautions at the right are numbered. Write the numbers below to show what each Caution means. (The first one is done for you.)

   6 Catches fire easily
   ___ Be sure there is a lot of fresh air
   ___ Don't breathe product
   ___ Don't throw empty can in garbage to be burned
   ___ Lock it up when not using it
   ___ Try not to get it on skin
   ___ If swallowed, see a doctor right away

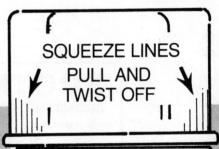

SQUEEZE LINES
PULL AND
TWIST OFF

ANT & ROACH KILLER

CAUTIONS

1. KEEP OUT OF REACH OF CHILDREN
2. HARMFUL IF INHALED
3. HARMFUL IF ABSORBED THROUGH SKIN
4. IF TAKEN INTERNALLY, CONTACT A PHYSICIAN IMMEDIATELY
5. PROVIDE ADEQUATE VENTILATION OF AREA BEING TREATED
6. FLAMMABLE
7. DO NOT INCINERATE CONTAINER

4. Drug Labels

READ the drug labels below.
NOTICE there are two kinds of drugs.
NOTICE the kinds of information on each.

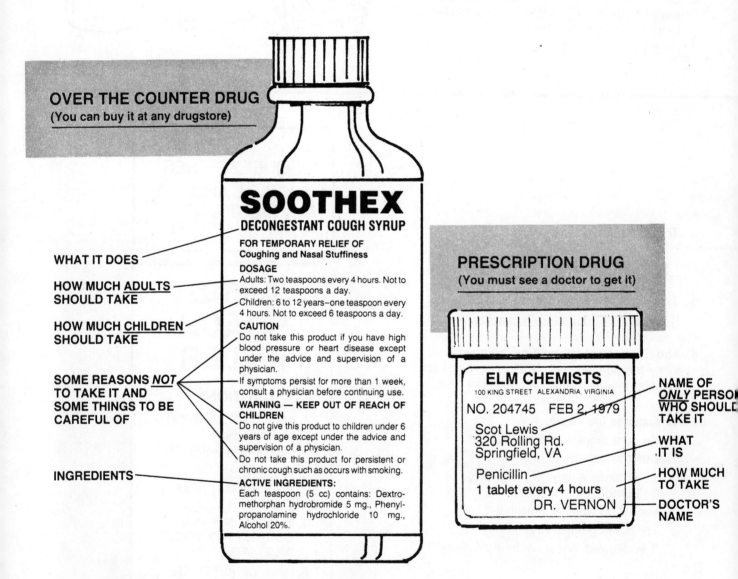

OVER THE COUNTER DRUG
(You can buy it at any drugstore)

SOOTHEX
DECONGESTANT COUGH SYRUP

FOR TEMPORARY RELIEF OF
Coughing and Nasal Stuffiness

DOSAGE
Adults: Two teaspoons every 4 hours. Not to exceed 12 teaspoons a day.
Children: 6 to 12 years–one teaspoon every 4 hours. Not to exceed 6 teaspoons a day.

CAUTION
Do not take this product if you have high blood pressure or heart disease except under the advice and supervision of a physician.
If symptoms persist for more than 1 week, consult a physician before continuing use.

WARNING — KEEP OUT OF REACH OF CHILDREN
Do not give this product to children under 6 years of age except under the advice and supervision of a physician.
Do not take this product for persistent or chronic cough such as occurs with smoking.

ACTIVE INGREDIENTS:
Each teaspoon (5 cc) contains: Dextromethorphan hydrobromide 5 mg., Phenylpropanolamine hydrochloride 10 mg., Alcohol 20%.

WHAT IT DOES

HOW MUCH ADULTS SHOULD TAKE

HOW MUCH CHILDREN SHOULD TAKE

SOME REASONS NOT TO TAKE IT AND SOME THINGS TO BE CAREFUL OF

INGREDIENTS

PRESCRIPTION DRUG
(You must see a doctor to get it)

ELM CHEMISTS
100 KING STREET ALEXANDRIA. VIRGINIA

NO. 204745   FEB 2, 1979

Scot Lewis
320 Rolling Rd.
Springfield, VA

Penicillin
1 tablet every 4 hours
DR. VERNON

NAME OF ONLY PERSON WHO SHOULD TAKE IT

WHAT IT IS

HOW MUCH TO TAKE

DOCTOR'S NAME

WORDS AND MEANINGS

dosage—how much of a drug to take and how often to take it

overdose—taking too much of a drug

symptoms—signs of sickness, such as a headache and fever

abrasions—places where skin is rubbed away

persists—keeps on

discontinue—stop

external—outside the body

antseptic—kills germs

decongestant—clears a stuffed-up nose

1. Look at the cough medicine on the last page. Where can you find how much to take?
   - [ ] Dosage
   - [ ] Warnings

2. You must see a doctor before getting
   - [ ] over-the-counter drugs
   - [ ] prescription drugs

3. How many teaspoons of cough medicine should an 8 year old child take?
   - [ ] 1 every 4 hours
   - [ ] 2 every 4 hours

4. Scot Lewis is taking the penicillin from Elm Chemists. He took a tablet at 12:00. When should he take the next tablet?
   - [ ] 1:00
   - [ ] 4:00
   - [ ] call Dr. Vernon to find out

5. Which symptom is a decongestant good for?
   - [ ] headache
   - [ ] stuffy nose

6. A label says **SEE PHYSICIAN IN CASE OF OVERDOSE.** What is an overdose?
   - [ ] needing more of a drug
   - [ ] taking more of the drug than directed

7. Who can take Soothex cough syrup without asking a doctor?
   - [ ] Mrs. Lopez, who has high blood presure and a cold
   - [ ] Mrs. Mosconi, who woke up with a cough and a stuffy nose
   - [ ] Mrs. Skofic, who coughs and coughs from smoking too much

8. Read the label on the VR-29 bottle (right). What should you do if you use VR-29 for several days and your cut still hurts?
   - [ ] use more of it
   - [ ] call a doctor

9. What does an antiseptic do?
   - [ ] kills germs
   - [ ] stops pain

10. Which is an abrasion?
    - [ ] deep cut
    - [ ] scrape

11. **FOR EXTERNAL USE ONLY** means that
    - [ ] put it on your skin
    - [ ] swallow it

VR-29

**ANTISEPTIC
FOR EXTERNAL USE ONLY**

For treatment of minor cuts and abrasions. Apply to injured area.

**CAUTION:
If redness, swelling
or pain persists,
call a physician.**

Unit 1 Review

These questions will help you review what you have learned about reading labels.

ANSWER each of the questions below. If you have trouble answering a question, it may help you to **LOOK BACK** in the lessons until you find the information you need.

1. **Do not incinerate** means
   - ☐ don't burn
   - ☐ don't drink
   - ☐ don't give to children

2. **Water repellent** means
   - ☐ almost waterproof
   - ☐ washable
   - ☐ waterproof

3. **If pain persists** means
   - ☐ if pain continues
   - ☐ if pain gets worse
   - ☐ if pain stops

4. **Net wt.** means
   - ☐ weight of contents
   - ☐ weight of package
   - ☐ weight of package and contents

5. **Colorfast** means
   - ☐ color fades fast
   - ☐ color comes out in the wash
   - ☐ color won't wash out

6. **Harmful if inhaled** means
   - ☐ don't breathe it in
   - ☐ don't get it on your skin
   - ☐ don't swallow it

7. **Flammable** means it
   - ☐ burns easily
   - ☐ irritates the skin
   - ☐ hurts your lungs

8. **For external use only** means
   - ☐ don't breathe it in
   - ☐ don't get it on your skin
   - ☐ don't swallow it

9. **50% polyester 50% cotton** means
   - ☐ the color may come out when you wash it
   - ☐ it's waterproof
   - ☐ you probably don't need to iron it after you wash it

10. **See a physician** means
    - ☐ get to a doctor
    - ☐ call a repairman
    - ☐ get to a druggist

11. **Nutrition information** on a food product label means facts about
    - ☐ weight and price
    - ☐ how to serve
    - ☐ how the body uses the food

12. **Ingredients** means
    - ☐ cautions
    - ☐ contents
    - ☐ dosage

13. **Permanent press** means
    - ☐ you don't have to wash it
    - ☐ you don't have to dry it
    - ☐ you don't have to iron it

14. **Provide adequate ventilation** means
    - ☐ call a doctor
    - ☐ do not swallow
    - ☐ open a window

15. **Dosage** means
    - ☐ how much to take
    - ☐ what a drug is used for
    - ☐ what to look out for

16. **A perishable** food means one that
    - ☐ contains many calories
    - ☐ has no artificial ingredients
    - ☐ spoils easily outside a refrigerator

Look at the labels to answer Questions 17-26.

17. Label 3 came from a shirt made mostly of
    □ cotton
    □ polyester and nylon

18. Which shirt is more likely to shrink?
    □ Label 3   □ Label 4

19. Which labels are on things that can be put in the washing machine? (Check more than one)
    □ 1   □ 2   □ 3   □ 4

20. Labels 4 and 5 are on dark green shirts. Which is on the shirt more likely to get green on the rest of the wash?
    □ Label 4   □ Label 5

21. Which is on the shirt most likely to need ironing?
    □ Label 3   □ Label 4   □ Label 5

22. What size is the shirt with Label 3?

    _____

23. Look at the label from a can of corn. List in the blanks what is in the can besides corn.

    1. _____

    2. _____

    3. _____

24. What is the net weight of this can of corn?

    _____ ounces

25. Which is not part of the net weight of this can of corn?
    □ can   □ corn   □ water

26. Murray is overweight. One cup of squash has 70 calories. Which will add less to Murray's weight?
    □ a cup of corn
    □ a cup of squash

WASH BLANKETS SEPARATELY
Use mild soap or detergent. Wash in lukewarm water—105F. Run machine 2-5 minutes. Rinse in cool water—two rinses. Use commercial fabric softener in final rinse. Tumble dry at medium temperature. Remove immediately from dryer. WPL 1675

LABEL 1

161 LAFAYETTE ST. N.Y.C.
DRY CLEAN ONLY

LABEL 2

Machine wash warm
Tumble dry
Remove promptly

42% Polyester
35% Nylon, 23% Cotton
Exclusive of Ornamentation
Rn 40361
LOT 2143S
STYLE 2433
SIZE: M

LABEL 3

MADE IN INDIA
100% COTTON
R.N. 52466
HAND WASH IN
COLD WATER

LABEL 4

WASHINGTON
DEE-CEE
WESTERN WEAR
PERMANENT PRESS
COLORFAST   MADE IN USA

LABEL 5

NUTRITION INFORMATION PER 1 CUP SERVING
Servings per container approximately 1 1/2 cups.
CALORIES 150
PROTEIN..4 grams
CARBOHYDRATE ....30 grams
FAT...1 gram
INGREDIENTS: Golden Whole Kernel Corn, Water, Sugar, Salt.
DIRECTIONS: Heat; Season to taste; Serve.
NET WT. 12 OZ.

LABEL FROM A CAN OF CORN

27. Which cottage cheese is fresher?
- ☐ one stamped "not to be sold after June 3"
- ☐ one stamped "not to be sold after June 6"

28. Look at the unit price labels. How much does one pound of this tuna fish cost?
- ☐ $1.46   ☐ $2.40

29. Look at Label 1. What should these tablets be used for?
- ☐ headache from a cold
- ☐ pain from a cut
- ☐ stomach feels awful from overeating

30. Read Label 1. How many tablets should be taken at one time?
- ☐ 1 or 2   ☐ 3 or 4

31. Read Label 1. Between 8 PM one night and 8 PM the next night you cannot take more than _____ tablets if you are an adult.

32. Read Label 1. How much should a child take?
- ☐ as much as needed
- ☐ half what an adult takes
- ☐ same as an adult takes

33. Who can use the prescription drug in Label 2?
- ☐ anyone who needs it
- ☐ only Bettina Fratelli

34. How should the medicine in Label 2 be used?
- ☐ only on the skin
- ☐ swallowed

35. Read Label 3. It is from a bottle of bleach. Check the <u>two</u> things you should do if some bleach gets in a person's eyes.
- ☐ call a doctor
- ☐ flood eyes with water
- ☐ give milk to the person

36. How much bleach should you use if you are washing a shirt by hand in 2 gallons of water?
- ☐ 1/8 cup   ☐ 1/2 cup   ☐ 1 cup

37. How much bleach should you use in a <u>regular</u> top-loading automatic?
- ☐ 1/8 cup   ☐ 1/2 cup   ☐ 1 cup

UNIT PRICE	YOU PAY
$2.40 per LB	$1.46 GREEN SEA TUNA 9.73 oz

For quick relief of **ACID INDIGESTION, SOUR STOMACH, OR HEARTBURN**
DIRECTIONS: Dissolve 1 **SELTZO-SOOTHE** tablet in a glass of water before taking. **ADULTS:** 1 or 2 tablets up to 8 tablets in a 24 hour period. **CHILDREN** 1/2 the adult dosage; or as directed by physician.
WARNINGS: Except under the advice and supervision of a physician,
Do not take more than: **ADULTS:** 8 tablets in a 24 hour period, **CHILDREN** 4 tablets in a 24 hour period.
Do not use the maximum dosage of this product for more than 2 weeks.
Do not use this product if you are on a sodium restricted diet. Each tablet contains 276 mg. of sodium.
Keep this and all drugs out of the reach of children.

LABEL 1

NEW PHARMACY
5380 SILVERADO TRAIL
CALISTOGA, CALIFORNIA

No. 421763   August 6, 1985

Bettina Fratelli
4217 Yount Street
Yountville, CA

Apply to affected area
4 times a day

FOR EXTERNAL USE ONLY

LABEL 2

CHLOR-WHITE BLEACH
CAUTION
KEEP OUT OF REACH OF CHILDREN
DIRECTIONS FOR USE
For best results, you should use the proper amount of bleach in the wash water. The guidelines below will provide excellent washing results.
- large top-loading automatic ....1-1/2 cups
- regular top-loading automatic....................1 cup
- front-loading automatic.........................1/2 cup
- hand laundry – 2 gallons of sudsy water .1/8 cup

CAUTION: Chlor-White may be harmful if swallowed or may cause severe eye irritation. If swallowed, feed milk. If splashed in eyes, flood with water. Call physician.

LABEL 3

Unit II.
FOLLOWING DIRECTIONS

A lot of Life Skills Reading is reading and following directions.

What happens if you don't read directions?

Viola Lambert didn't slow down when a sign told her to. She landed in a hospital. She was sued by the owner of the car she hit. She has huge car repair bills. And she lost her driver's license.

Roberto Moseati parked where a sign told him not to. The police gave him a ticket and towed away his car. It cost him $75 to get it back.

Angel Gutierrez spends more than $75 a week to eat in restaurants. He says he can't save money because he doesn't know how to cook.

Gail Burden had to paint the steps all over again. She mixed the paint wrong the first time.

Gerard Van Allen didn't qualify for the job he wanted. He knew most of the answers on the test. But he didn't follow directions, and he marked his answers in the wrong spaces.

CONTENTS OF THIS UNIT

5. Road Signs

READ Road Signs to stay out of danger.
NOTICE that different kinds of signs have different shapes.

STOP

WARNING

INFORMATION

RAILROAD AND OTHER SPECIAL SIGNS

WORDS AND MEANINGS

merge—two lanes of traffic must squeeze into one lane

intersection—place where two roads cross

detour—another road to take when the regular one has something wrong with it

pedestrian—person who is walking

proceed—go on ahead

caution—being careful

construction—road work or work on a building

prohibited—you are not allowed to do it

QUESTIONS

1. A sign with 8 sides always means:
   ☐ slow ☐ stop

2. A sign tells you **DANGER FALLING ROCKS.** Which shape should it have?

   ☐ ◇ ☐ ☐

3. The sign with the abbreviation for railroad warns that trains might cross. What is the abbreviation?
   ☐ **RA** ☐ **RD** ☐ **RR**

4. **PROCEED WITH CAUTION** means:
   ☐ go carefully
   ☐ stop

5. The road is all torn up for repairs. Which sign would you see?

☐ 1   ☐ 2

6. Cars go very fast on this highway. There is no safe place to walk. Which sign would you see?

☐ 2   ☐ 3   ☐ 4

7. A hill makes it hard to see where Ox Road crosses Fox Road. Which sign would you see?

☐ 1   ☐ 2   ☐ 3

8. Which sign tells you to start looking for a chance to pull into the left lane?

☐ 2   ☐ 3   ☐ 5

9. Which sign tells you not to take the usual road?

☐ 3   ☐ 4   ☐ 5

SLOW
DANGEROUS
INTERSECTION

1

PROCEED
WITH CAUTION
CONSTRUCTION
NEXT
5
MILES

2

DETOUR

3

PEDESTRIANS
PROHIBITED

4

5 MERGE LEFT
RIGHT LANE ENDS
500 FEET

10. The arrows show where the cars are going. Which picture shows the driver obeying the sign?

☐ 1   ☐ 2

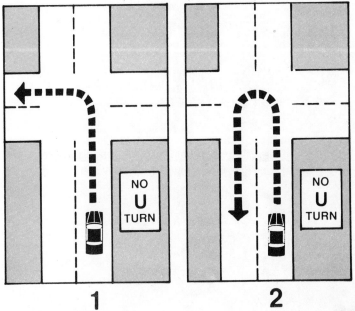

NO
U
TURN

1

NO
U
TURN

2

6. Signs Around Town

_S A__ MEANINGS

—sitt___ ___ with the motor running

throw___ ___ away instead of putting

___ca__

___with ___ ___on

___cars, tru___ etc.

ing—e___t___a place where you are

___d

___ed—not ___ed

___one—___ reserved for trucks and vans

___e—cat___ on fire easily

___ion—c___ ___

___STION__

___h tells yo___ ___ stop even if

___ your car___

☐ 2

___ ___ likely ___ ___on a gasoline

☐ 5

___ warn___ ___ ___ to throw a paper

___ ___ stree__

☐ 5

___ ___ ___ ___ of a parking

___ ___part __

☐ ___

___ warns ___ against parking where

___ their pic___ps and deliveries?

☐ 2   ☐ ___

___ you p___ ___ to Sign 1?

___hursda___ ___

___ursd___

___nda__

Sign	Text
1	NO PARKING 11AM–2PM TUES-THURS-SAT Dept. of Traffic
2	NO PARKING LOADING ZONE
3	BUS STOP / NO STANDING
4	NO TRESPASSING AUTHORIZED VEHICLES ONLY
5	LITTERING PROHIBITED
6	HIGHLY FLAMMABLE

7. Is the car in the left lane obeying the signs?

☐ yes   ☐ no

8. Is the car in the right lane obeying the signs?

☐ yes   ☐ no

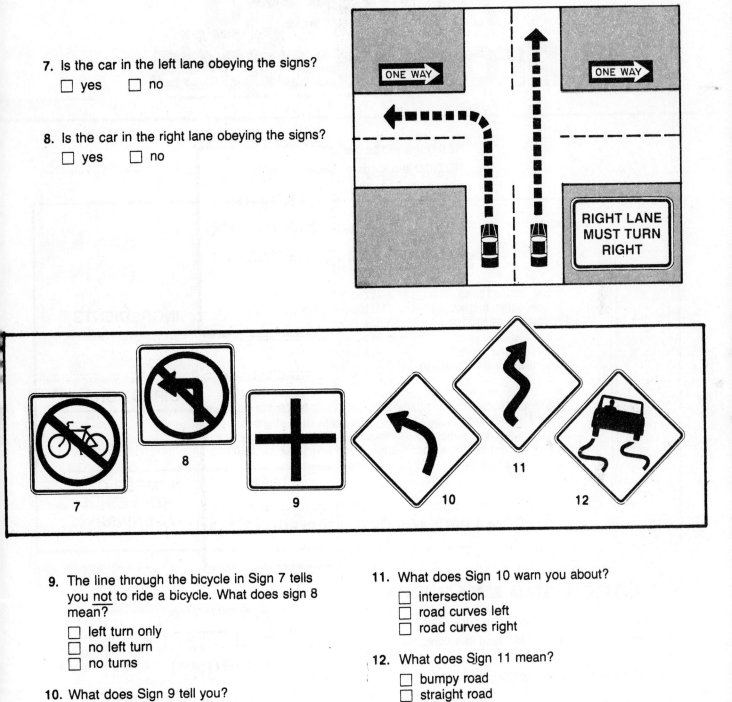

9. The line through the bicycle in Sign 7 tells you <u>not</u> to ride a bicycle. What does sign 8 mean?

☐ left turn only
☐ no left turn
☐ no turns

10. What does Sign 9 tell you?

☐ curve ahead
☐ intersection ahead
☐ no turns

11. What does Sign 10 warn you about?

☐ intersection
☐ road curves left
☐ road curves right

12. What does Sign 11 mean?

☐ bumpy road
☐ straight road
☐ winding road

13. Sign 12 tells you if the road is wet, it may be:

☐ closed
☐ flooded
☐ slippery

7. Cooking From Recipes

READ the recipe below.
NOTICE the kinds of information.

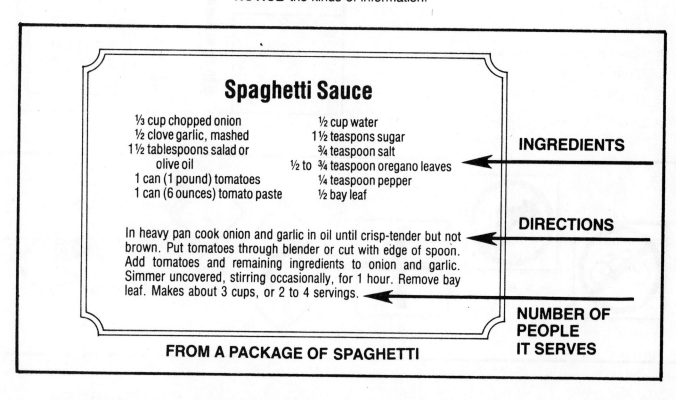

Spaghetti Sauce

⅓ cup chopped onion
½ clove garlic, mashed
1½ tablespoons salad or
 olive oil
1 can (1 pound) tomatoes
1 can (6 ounces) tomato paste

½ cup water
1½ teaspons sugar
¾ teaspoon salt
½ to ¾ teaspoon oregano leaves
¼ teaspoon pepper
½ bay leaf

← INGREDIENTS

In heavy pan cook onion and garlic in oil until crisp-tender but not brown. Put tomatoes through blender or cut with edge of spoon. Add tomatoes and remaining ingredients to onion and garlic. Simmer uncovered, stirring occasionally, for 1 hour. Remove bay leaf. Makes about 3 cups, or 2 to 4 servings.

← DIRECTIONS

← NUMBER OF PEOPLE IT SERVES

FROM A PACKAGE OF SPAGHETTI

WORDS AND MEANINGS

simmer—bring to a boil and cook over low heat
shortening—a solid fat used in baking, like butter or lard
preheat—heat oven before you use it

oregano—an herb (a plant leaf) used to give flavor in many Italian foods
sifted—passed through a sifter (a cup with screens on the bottom). This gets rid of lumps in flour and makes it fluffy. If you don't have a sifter, do this with a large strainer

QUESTIONS

1. You don't have the things below. Which should you get before making the spaghetti sauce?

☐ oregano.   ☐ eggs

2. To make 6 cups of spaghetti sauce, double everything in the recipe. How many servings will 6 cups give?

☐ 2 to 4
☐ 4 to 8

3. In a recipe, 1 cup means 1 measuring cup. Which arrow shows how high to fill the cup with water for the spaghetti sauce?

☐ A   ☐ B   ☐ C

1 CUP — A
¾
½ — B
¼ — C

MEASURING CUP

4. **tbsp** = tablespoon   **tsp** = teaspoon

Which is bigger?

☐ 1 tbsp   ☐ 1 tsp

5. Draw a circle around the spoon to be used to measure pepper for the sauce.

1 TABLESPOON

1 TEASPOON

½ TEASPOON

¼ TEASPOON

MEASURING SPOONS

6. Which do you cook first?

☐ onion and garlic
☐ tomatoes and spices

7. Add the tomatoes, then cook the sauce over:

☐ low heat
☐ high heat

8. Read this cornbread recipe. When is the best time to light the oven?

☐ after everything is mixed
☐ before you start

9. Sifted flour is:

☐ light   ☐ lumpy

10. Which can you use for the shortening in the cornbread?

☐ cream
☐ margarine

GOLDEN YELLOW CORNBREAD

1 cup Yellow Corn
      Meal
1 cup sifted flour
¼ cup sugar
3 teaspoons baking
    powder

1 teaspon salt
¼ cup soft shortening
1 cup milk
1 egg, beaten
<u>Preheat oven to 425 F.</u>

Combine corn meal, flour, sugar, baking powder and salt in a bowl. Cut in shortening. Mix egg and milk together and add to dry ingredients with a few swift strokes. Bake in greased 9 x 9 x 2 inch pan for 20 to 25 minutes.

**FROM A PACKAGE OF
CORN MEAL**

8. Product Instructions

Instructions on how to use a product are often printed on a box label or in a separate owner's manual.

You should read the instructions from start to finish before you use the product. Be sure you:

1. Understand each step.
2. Understand the order (what to do first, second, etc.)
3. Have everything you need.

READ the box label below until you understand the instructions.

WORDS AND MEANINGS

consistency—thickness of a mixture

excess—extra

spackling compound—a powder made of plaster, glue, and rock dust and used to fix cracks.

owner's manual—a booklet that comes with something you buy and tells you how to use it

QUESTIONS

1. What <u>don't</u> you need to fill in the crack with Crackle?

   ☐ something to mix it in
   ☐ screwdriver
   ☐ sandpaper
   ☐ putty knife

2. Luis Campos never used Crackle before. He has no idea of how much water to add. What should he do?

   ☐ mix in a little water at a time until all lumps disappear
   ☐ add a lot of water and see what happens

3. You bought this Fast-Fix Epoxy to fix a broken bowl. What don't you need?

☐ a pin
☐ sandpaper
☐ something to mix it on
☐ something to mix it with

4. Ada squeezed out 2 inches of epoxy and 1 inch of hardener. What should she do next?

☐ mix the two
☐ squeeze out more epoxy
☐ squeeze out more hardener

5. What is the step <u>after</u> squeezing out equal lengths from each tube?

☐ mixing hardener and epoxy
☐ putting epoxy on bowl

6. You put the pieces of the bowl together. There are some blobs of epoxy on the bowl. What should you do?

☐ let them dry
☐ wipe them away

7. You got a little epoxy on your hands. What should you do?

☐ call a doctor
☐ wash with soap and water

8. You have a new car. You want to find out how often to change the oil. Where should you look?

In the _____
(fill in blank)

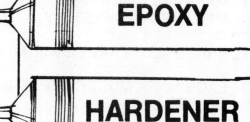

NEW
FAST FIX
EPOXY
FOR SUPER FAST REPAIRS STRONGER THAN GLUE

EPOXY

HARDENER

DIRECTIONS

1. STICK A PIN INTO THE ENDS OF BOTH TUBES

2. SQUEEZE EQUAL LENGTHS OF EPOXY AND HARDENER ONTO CLEAN DISCARDABLE SURFACE

3. MIX THOROUGHLY

4. CLEAN AND DRY SURFACE TO BE REPAIRED

5. APPLY AND WIPE AWAY EXCESS BEFORE HARDENING. HARDENS IN 6 MINUTES

CAUTION: MAY CAUSE SKIN IRRITATION. WASH WITH SOAP AND WATER. SEE PHYSICIAN IF TAKEN INTERNALLY. KEEP OUT OF REACH OF CHILDREN.

9. Taking A Test

Many tests are graded by machines.
Machines think stray pencil marks are mistakes.
On the Answer Sheet below, only Answer 1 would
be read correctly by the machine.

ANSWER SHEET

DIRECTIONS

1. MAKE ONLY ONE MARK TO ANSWER ONE ITEM. ERASE ALL MISTAKES COMPLETELY.

2. ERASE ALL STRAY PENCIL MARKS

3. EACH MARK MUST COMPLETELY FILL THE SPACE BETWEEN THE DOTTED LINES.

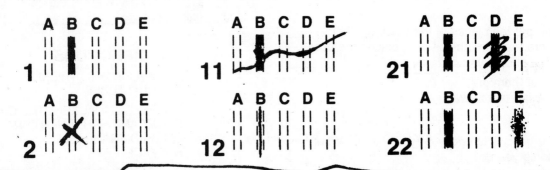

WORDS AND MEANINGS

preceding—just before
glossy—shiny

position—job
initial—first letter of a name

QUESTIONS

1. Find Answer 2 above. Which direction on the answer sheet was not followed? (Choose one of the numbered directions on the sheet.)

   ☐ 1   ☐ 2   ☐ 3

2. Find Answer 11. Which direction was not followed?

   ☐ 1   ☐ 2   ☐ 3

3. Find Answer 12. Which direction was not followed?

   ☐ 1   ☐ 2   ☐ 3

4. Find Answers 21 and 22. Which direction was not followed?

   ☐ 1   ☐ 2   ☐ 3

5. Write your name on the Answer Sheet at the bottom of this page. Be careful which name you put first.

6. Fill in today's date on the Answer Sheet. The test is for a job as a clerk/typist. Fill that in.

Answer Questions 7 and 8 on the Answer Sheet below.

7. DIRECTIONS —TEST QUESTION 27

In the sentence below, choose the letter preceding the word that most nearly matches the meaning of the underlined word. Mark the space under that letter on the Answer Sheet. Be sure you are in the right place for Answer 27.

Lions are giant cats.

A. animals
B. big
C. scary
D. small
E. ugly

8. DIRECTIONS —TEST QUESTION 28

In the problem below, mark the answer with the same letter as the correct answer if the correct answer is given. If it is not given, fill in the space under the E on the Answer Sheet. Be sure you are in the right place for Answer 28.

50¢ plus 5¢ equals:

A. 1¢
B. $5
C. $10
D. $100
E. none of the above

ANSWER SHEET

TEST NO. 26-18-N

NAME: _____ _____ _____
　　　　　　LAST　　　　　　FIRST　　　　INITIAL

DATE _____

POSITION _____

MAKE ONLY ONE MARK FOR EACH ANSWER. MAKE GLOSSY BLACK MARKS.

	A B C D E		A B C D E		A B C D E		A B C D E
1	‖ ‖ ‖ ‖ ‖	26	‖ ‖ ‖ ‖ ‖	51	‖ ‖ ‖ ‖ ‖	76	‖ ‖ ‖ ‖ ‖
2	‖ ‖ ‖ ‖ ‖	27	‖ ‖ ‖ ‖ ‖	52	‖ ‖ ‖ ‖ ‖	77	‖ ‖ ‖ ‖ ‖
3	‖ ‖ ‖ ‖ ‖	28	‖ ‖ ‖ ‖ ‖	53	‖ ‖ ‖ ‖ ‖	78	‖ ‖ ‖ ‖ ‖
4	‖ ‖ ‖ ‖ ‖	29	‖ ‖ ‖ ‖ ‖	54	‖ ‖ ‖ ‖ ‖	79	‖ ‖ ‖ ‖ ‖
5	‖ ‖ ‖ ‖ ‖	30	‖ ‖ ‖ ‖ ‖	55	‖ ‖ ‖ ‖ ‖	80	‖ ‖ ‖ ‖ ‖

Unit 2 Review

1. **Merge Right** means
   - ☐ follow the road as it curves right
   - ☐ move into the right lane
   - ☐ turn right

2. An example of **shortening** is
   - ☐ butter
   - ☐ eggs
   - ☐ flour

3. **Detour** means
   - ☐ be careful of road work
   - ☐ move into another lane
   - ☐ take a different road

4. **Tbsp** means
   - ☐ tables
   - ☐ tablespoon
   - ☐ teaspoon

5. **Vehicles Prohibited** means
   - ☐ drive this way
   - ☐ do not walk here
   - ☐ do not drive here

6. The page **preceding** page 22 is
   - ☐ page 21
   - ☐ page 22
   - ☐ page 23

7. **Proceed With Caution** means
   - ☐ go ahead carefully
   - ☐ speed up
   - ☐ stop

8. James Anthony Rocco's middle **initial** is
   - ☐ A
   - ☐ Anthony
   - ☐ Tony

9. When you apply for a **position** it means you're
   - ☐ asking for a job
   - ☐ asking a question
   - ☐ trying to get in line

10. **Excess** water is water that is
    - ☐ inside
    - ☐ outside
    - ☐ too much

11. **Simmer** means
    - ☐ bake at high heat
    - ☐ cook in liquid over low heat
    - ☐ fry at medium heat

12. Which is the largest measure?
    - ☐ cup
    - ☐ tablespoon
    - ☐ teaspoon

13. **Intersection** means
    - ☐ dangerous road over train tracks
    - ☐ road curving
    - ☐ roads crossing

14. **No Trespassing** means
    - ☐ don't apply there
    - ☐ don't enter there
    - ☐ don't throw things there

15. **Sifting** flour means
    - ☐ heating it gently over low heat
    - ☐ packing it down tight
    - ☐ shaking it through a large strainer

16. **Preheat** oven means
    - ☐ do not heat oven
    - ☐ heat oven before putting food in
    - ☐ put food in, then turn on oven

17. A **pedestrian** is
    - ☐ a driver
    - ☐ a passenger
    - ☐ a walker

28

Answer Questions 18-24 by looking at the signs.

18. Which sign can you park next to at 4PM Saturday?
    - ☐ Sign 1
    - ☐ Sign 2
    - ☐ neither of the above

19. Can you sit in your car next to Sign 1 and wait for a friend?
    - ☐ yes   ☐ no

20. Which sign tells you not to turn left?
    - ☐ Sign 3   ☐ Sign 4   ☐ Sign 5

21. Which sign tells you the road curves a lot?
    - ☐ Sign 3   ☐ Sign 4   ☐ Sign 5

22. Which sign tells you there is an intersection ahead?
    - ☐ Sign 4   ☐ Sign 5   ☐ Sign 6

23. What does Sign 6 mean?

    _____

24. What does Sign 7 mean?
    - ☐ you can't drive there
    - ☐ you can't walk there
    - ☐ you can't throw anything away there

Read the recipe to answer Questions 25-28.

25. What is the first step in baking Oatmeal Raisin cookies?
    - ☐ light the oven
    - ☐ mix shortening and sugar, eggs and vanilla
    - ☐ sift flour with other ingredients

26. How much salt do you need?
    - ☐ 1/2 tsp   ☐ 1 tsp   ☐ 1 tbsp

27. Which does not get sifted in with the flour?
    - ☐ baking soda
    - ☐ salt
    - ☐ sugar

28. After you beat the shortening, sugar, eggs, and vanilla until fluffy, what do you do next?
    - ☐ add raisins
    - ☐ add flour mixture and oats
    - ☐ spoon mixture onto cookie sheets

OATMEAL-RAISIN COOKIES

1-1/2 cups sifted all-purpose
1 teaspoon baking soda
1 teaspoon salt
1 cup shortening
1 cup granulated sugar
1 cup light brown sugar, firmly packed
2 eggs
1 teaspoon vanilla extract
3 cups raw, quick-cooking oats
1 cup seedless raisins

1. Preheat oven to 375F. Lightly grease cookie
2. Sift flour, baking soda and
3. In a large bowl, with electric mixer at medium
   or wooden spoon, beat shortening, sugars, and
   vanilla until light and fluffy.
4. Add flour mixture and oats with wooden
   until well blended. Stir in
5. With hands, roll into balls, or use slightly rounded
   tablespoonful for each. Place cookies apart, on
   prepared cookie sheets.
6. Bake 12 to 14 minutes, or until golden brown.
   stand 1 minute, then remove to rack, cool
   about 2-1/2 dozen.

Read the instructions to the right, for using a glass cutter. Then answer Questions 29-30.

29. Katerina wants to cut a piece of glass to fix a broken window. What should she do after she cleans the glass?

☐ lay it on a table
☐ lay it on a table, but raise one end a little
☐ stand it on end

30. The glass cutter does not cut clear through the glass. It only scratches it. After you cut a scratch into the glass, what is the next step?

☐ break the glass right away by bending it
☐ cut a second scratch into the glass
☐ turn the glass over and cut a scratch on the other side

Answer the question below on the Answer Sheet at the bottom of this page.

31. Fill out the top part of the Answer Sheet. Print your own name and use today's date. The job you are trying to get is fire fighter. Fill this in on the Answer Sheet.

   Read the Directions below and answer the question.

   DIRECTIONS: Read the beginning of the sentence below. Pay close attention to the underlined word. Choose the word that best completes the sentence. Notice the letter next to that word, and mark the space under that letter on the Answer Sheet. Be sure you find Answer 1.

   QUESTION 1

   An **apple** is a
     A book   **D** orange
     B dog   **E** tool
     C fruit

TO CUT GLASS EASILY

Wipe glass clean. Lay glass on flat surface. Dip wheel in light oil. Hold cutter upright between first and second fingers.

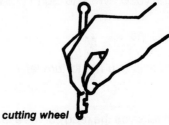

cutting wheel

To get feel, make practice cuts on scrap glass. Use a straight edge and start cut 1/16 inch from farthest edge.

Avoid excessive pressure.

Draw cutter across pane with a firm continuous stroke. Allow wheel to drop off edge of pane. Break glass immediately by holding glass between the first finger and thumb of both hands and giving the glass a slight bend.

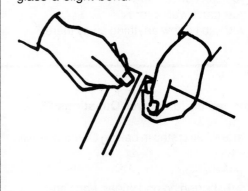

ANSWER SHEET

TEST NO. __402__   NAME: _____
                        LAST   FIRST   INITIAL

DATE _____   POSITION _____

MAKE ONLY ONE MARK FOR EACH ANSWER. MAKE GLOSSY BLACK MARKS.

	A B C D E		A B C D E		A B C D E		A B C D E
1	A B C D E	**26**	A B C D E	**51**	A B C D E	**76**	A B C D E
	A B C D E		A B C D		A B C D E		A B C D E

Unit III.
LOOKING UP INFORMATION

One of the most important skills in Life Skills Reading is being able to find a piece of information rapidly and accurately.

If you're looking for information in a book, you need to use the Table of Contents and the Index. And you need to know the differences between them.

If you don't want to miss something on TV, you need to know how to read TV program listings.

If you want to get a job or find a place to live, you'd better learn how to use newspaper ads.

The dictionary gives you information about words or meanings—if you know how to use it.

The phone book and the Yellow Pages are a valuable key to making phone calls or doing shopping—if you know how to find and use their information.

You need to know how to use timetables if you ride on trains, planes, or buses. You need to be able to look things up in a street map when you're in a strange part of town or in a city different from the one you live in.

You may need to look something up almost every day of your life.

CONTENTS OF THIS UNIT

10. Finding the Right Page
11. Finding What's On TV
12. Using Classified Ads
13. Finding Jobs in Want Ads
14. Using the Dictionary
15. Using the Phone Book
16. Using the Yellow Pages
17. Reading Timetables
18. Reading Street Maps

10. Finding The Right Page

Both the **Table of Contents** and the **Index** below are from the same book, Home Repair.

NOTICE what they tell you and how they are different.

WORDS AND MEANINGS

Glossary—list of difficult words with their meanings

Table of contents—at the front of a book. Lists general contents by chapters

Index—at the back of a book. Lists detailed contents alphabetically

Quick Index—Index in a mail order catalog with only the main kinds of goods listed

General Index—Index in a mail order catalog that lists specific items

QUESTIONS

1. You can quickly learn a lot about a book by reading the names of the chapters. Which is good for this?
   ☐ Index
   ☐ Table of Contents

2. Which contains items in alphabetical order?
   ☐ Index
   ☐ Table of Contents

3. Which comes near the beginning of the book?
   ☐ Index
   ☐ Table of Contents

4. Which might be in the Glossary?
   ☐ how to fix a leak
   ☐ meaning of lag bolt

5. Write <u>TC</u> next to the example where you should look in the Table of Contents. Write <u>I</u> next to the example where you should look in the Index.
   _____You want to find out how to <u>turn off the water</u>
   _____You want to read about <u>plumbing</u>

6. You don't need to read the whole chapter on Electricity to find out how to change a light switch. You can find the right page by looking up <u>switch</u> in the
   ☐ Index
   ☐ Table of Contents

7. Mail Order Catalogs have no Table of Contents. Sometimes they have a Quick Index instead.

   Eric wants to add some electrical appliances to his kitchen but he doesn't know for sure which ones he wants. Where in the catalog should he look first?
   ☐ General Index
   ☐ Quick Index

8. Graciela wants to order an electric fryer. Where in the catalog should she look to find one?
   ☐ General Index
   ☐ Quick Index

9. Newspapers have an Index on the 1st or 2nd page and no Table of Contents. Part of a newspaper Index is at the right.

   Where would you look to see what movies were playing?

   pages _____
   (fill in)

PART OF A QUICK INDEX

Appliances	72-85
Children's Clothes	10-60
Games	105-135
Men's Clothes	250-302
Musical Instruments	310-331
Sporting Goods	136-160

PART OF A GENERAL INDEX

Flashlights	180
Flutes	312
Food Grinders	77
Football Equipment	140, 143
Fryers, Electric	75
Games	105-135

INDEX

Amusements	20-25
Classified Ads	26-28
Comics	29-30
Dear Abby	30
Editorials	9-10
Financial	31-33

11. Finding What's On TV

Below is the evening part of the TV information from The Washington Post.

NOTICE that all the shows that begin at 8:00 are listed straight across from 8:00. All the shows on Channel 4 are listed under the 4.

1/30	4 NBC WRC	5 WTTG	7 ABC WJLA	9 CBS WDVM	20 WDCA	22 PBS WAPB	26 PBS WETA	53 ♠14 WNVT
6 :00 :30	Jim Vance Willard Scott NBC News	Andy Griffith (R) Six Million Dollar	News	News w/ Gordon Peterson M. Bunyan	The Bionic Woman (R) "Motorcycle Boogie"	Tomorrow's Families Introduction to Math (R)	Studio See Congressional Outlook	Villa Alegre Studio See
7 :00 :30	Newlywed Game Hollywood Squares	Man (R) Dating Game	ABC News Tic Tac Dough	CBS News $25,000 Pyramid	Sanford and Son (R) Hockey Washington	MacNeil/Lehrer Report Medix "Heart Attack"	Over Easy MacNeil/Lehrer Report	Lilias, Yoga and You Over Easy
8 :00 :30	Mark Twain's America: "Young Abe Lincoln"	Match Game PM Donna Fargo	Happy Days (R) Laverne & Shirley	Response to State of Union 8:40, Report on Chinese Visit	Capitals vs. Detroit Red Wings	Masterpiece Theater (R) "Duchess of Duke Street"	Julia Child and Company Wodehouse Playhouse	National Geographic "Hong Kong"
9 :00 :30	Movie "The Triangle Factory Fire Scandal"	Merv Griffin w/ Zsa Zsa Gabor George Miller	Three's Company (R) Taxi (R)	Movie "Big Jake" ('76) stars John Wayne		The Energy War part 2	The Energy War part 3	Virginia Legislature The Energy War part 2
10 :00 :30	('78) stars Tom Bosley Tovah Feldshuh	News w/ Paul Udell Delores Handy	Starsky and Hutch (R)	Richard Boone Maureen O'Hara	Hogan's Heroes (R)	In Person		
11 :00 :30	News w/ Hartz & Vance Tonight Show (R) w/ Johnny	Odd Couple Perry Mason w/ Raymond	News ABC News Close-Up	News w/ J. C. Hayward Barnaby Jones (R)	Twilight Zone (R)	Dick Cavett w/ Lillian Gish Captioned ABC News	Dick Cavett w/ Lillian Gish Captioned ABC World News	
12 :00 :30	Carson Lana Cantrell 1, Tomorrow	Burr (R) "Three Comrades"	"Mission: Mind Control"	Movie	The PTL Club 1, Untouchables			

WORDS AND MEANINGS

vs—versus, playing against in sports
w/—with

R—repeat or rerun

QUESTIONS

1. How many movies are on at 9 o'clock?

2. Which movie has John Wayne in it?
  ☐ The Triangle Factory Fire
  ☐ Big Jake

3. Starsky & Hutch is on at 10:00. Could you have seen this one before?
  ☐ yes   ☐ no

4. At which time are most of the news programs?
  ☐ 9:00   ☐ 10:00   ☐ 11:00

5. What time does the hockey game start?

_____
(write on line)

6. What channel is it on?
Channel _____

7. What time does it end? (Same time as Hogan's Heroes begins)

_____

8. What abbreviation means against?

_____

9. What team is the Washington Capitals playing against?

_____

10. News w/ Paul Udell means:
☐ news watch by Paul Udell
☐ news with Paul Udell

11. Shows may be divided into parts and the parts shown on different nights. Notice Energy War at 9:00. Can you see the whole program in one night?

☐ yes   ☐ no

---

12. At the right is the TV Information from the <u>Portland Press Herald</u>. The channel numbers are in little TV screens listed under the times. How many channels show The Waltons at 8:00?

_____

13. This paper marks the movies it thinks are great with 4 stars. Which movie seems better?
☐ Spy Who Came in from the Cold (at 8:00)
☐ Colombo: Requiem for a Falling Star (at 12:05)

8:00

② ④ ⑥ Legends Of The Superheroes — The Roast
An assortment of comic book heroes including Captain Marvel, Batman and Robin and, the Huntress gathers to be "roasted" by a group of villains and other heroes.

⑤ ⑦ ⑧ Mork & Mindy
Mork tries to free Eugene and his little girlfriend from parental persecution by performing their wedding ceremony.

⑤ ⑦ ⑬ The Waltons
Jim-Bob decides to become a minister after an accident causes him to re-evaluate his life.

⑨ Le Travail a la Chaine

⑩ ⑫ ㉖ Nova
"The Mind Machines" Who - or what - will take over when computers begin to think better than their creators? (R)

⑪ Garden Show

⑤⑥ Movie
★★★½ "Spy Who Came In From The Cold" (1966) Richard Burton, Claire Bloom. A British spy is assigned to track down a Communist spy responsible for ruining many intelligence missions. (2 hrs., 30 min.)

11:30

② ④ ⑥ Tonight
Guest host: Rich Little. Guest: McLean Stevenson.

⑤ ⑦ ⑧ Starsky & Hutch
Starsky and Hutch are suspected of shooting an innocent bystander who was the wife of a government agent. (R)

⑤ ⑦ ⑬ M*A*S*H
Hawkeye and Trapper John help an enlisted Korean get a pass to see his pregnant wife. (R)

⑩ ⑫ ㉖ Captioned ABC News

㊳ The Rifleman
"Jailbird"

⑤⑥ Love, American Style
"Love And The Other Love" Pat has always considered her husband not only sweet but sane, then he buys a sports car.

12:00

㊳ The Rifleman
"Jealous Man"

12:05

⑤ ⑦ ⑬ CBS Late Movie
★★½ "Columbo: Requiem For A Falling Star" (1972) Peter Falk, Anne Baxter.

12:37

⑤ ⑦ ⑧ Mannix

12. Using Classified Ads

You can find cars, jobs, apartments, and more in the Classified Ads in your paper. An Index will help you find the section you want.

NOTICE 700-799 Rentals in the Index. This section has apartments to rent.

NOTICE in the ads that Furnished and Unfurnished apartments are listed separately.

NOTICE that apartments inside the city of Washington, D.C. and those in nearby Maryland (Md) are listed separately.

CLASSIFIED INDEX

700-799 RENTALS

**708
APTS FURN, D.C.**

FOGGY BOTTOM, small 1 BR adults, no pets $250 + utils good location 431-2691

DOWNTOWN, 6th St, cozy effcy, $35 wk, 393-1617

**720
APTS FURN, MD.**

OXEN HILL, Spotless 1BR, full modern kitchen, $255, weekends 298-7073

**722
APTS UNFURN, MD.**

ADELPHI, 2 BR, garden, w-w cpt, avail Apr 1 $190 + utils, 721-1418

CHEVY CHASE, mod kit. 1 & 2 BR apts fr. $210, sec. dep req. refs req. 682-0062

LANHAM, 1 BR, just painted $150 + utils, parking avail. 434-5217

SILVER SPRING, Univ. Blvd. 1 BR, $165 incl. utils. eat in kit. conv. trans. 434-5510

WORDS AND MEANINGS

sec. dep. req.—security deposit required. You pay the landlord money which is returned when you move out, only if you didn't harm anything in the apartment.

fr $210—from $210, $210 is the cheapest rent; others are more

refs. req.—references required. Someone must write that you pay your bills on time or that you will be good to rent to

effcy.—efficiency, 1 room apartment with tiny kitchen

conv. trans.—convenient to transportation, close to buses or subways

+ utils—plus utilities (electricity, gas, water). These are extra, and are not included in the rent

utils. incl.—utilities included in the rent. Landlord pays them

w-w cpt.—wall to wall carpets

avail—available

BR—bedroom

Real Estate—land or building for sale

QUESTIONS

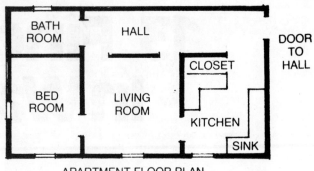

APARTMENT FLOOR PLAN

1. Which apartment mentioned in the ads could this floor plan be for? (Both have living rooms, though the ads don't say so)
   - [ ] the one in Lanham
   - [ ] the one in Silver Spring

2. Mona wants an apartment with furniture in Maryland. How many apartments like this are listed?
   - [ ] 1   [ ] 2   [ ] 3   [ ] 4

3. How many bedrooms are in the apartment in Foggy Bottom?
   - [ ] 1   [ ] 2   [ ] 3 or 4

4. In which apartment will you have to pay extra for gas and electricity?
   - [ ] the one in Lanham
   - [ ] the one in Silver Spring

5. Les has no car. He takes the bus. Which apartment sounds better for him?
   - [ ] the one in Lanham
   - [ ] the one in Silver Spring

6. Which ad says someone must write about what you are like before you can get the apartment?
   - [ ] the one in Adelphi
   - [ ] the one in Chevy Chase

7. The place in Chevy Chase has more than one apartment available. $210 a month is
   - [ ] the cheapest rent
   - [ ] the highest rent

8. Will the landlord in Chevy Chase want more than $210 before you get the apartment?
   - [ ] yes   [ ] no

9. When do you get the security deposit back?
   - [ ] never
   - [ ] when you move out

10. Ella wants wall-to-wall carpeting. Which apartment has this?
    - [ ] the one in Adelphi
    - [ ] the one in Chevy Chase

11. Today is March 10. Can you move into the apartment in Adelphi right away?
    - [ ] yes   [ ] no

12. Lori Castro wants to own her own house. Where should she look?
    - [ ] 700-799 Rentals
    - [ ] 800-899 Real Estate

13. Finding Jobs In Want Ads

In the Classified Index the heading "Employment" will help you find the "Help Wanted" section where companies advertise for employees.

NOTICE below, the ads are in alphabetical order.

NOTICE each ad usually says:

--what skills they need
--what they offer
--what you should do if you are interested

HELP WANTED	HELP WANTED
1 — **CLERK TYPISTS** Expd clerks to help w/ filing and typing, 55 wpm, top pay and benefits. Apply in person 1-4 pm, Transit Corp. 354 W. Touhy, Lincolnwood	**GENERAL OFFICE** Must type 45 w.p.m., nice phone personality, congenial office, call 922-6732 — **5**
2 — **CLERK TYPIST** General office exp. type 65 wpm. Permanent full time. Excellent salary and fringe benefits. Call Mrs Stevens, 280-2034	**MANAGER-ASSISTANT** Mens clothing store, South Chicago area, prefer bilingual Spanish-English. Exp. helpful but not necessary. Call Mr. Lewis for appt., 768-5320 — **6**
3 — **CRANE OPERATOR** Expd only. Salary commensurate with exp. Send resume to Box MPZ 247 Tribune 60611	**SALES** Will train, hifi, audio, TV good salary and benefits. Ask for Howard, 753-8205 — **7**
4 — **DRIVERS** Deliver to hospitals, flexible hours. Must have valid driver's license, car provided, 732-4177	**SALES PERSON** Carpets, expanding store, exp'd, good salary plus com mission, 823-7830. — **8**

WORDS AND MEANINGS

exp, expd—experience, experienced

fringe benefits—extras the company gives you besides your salary

congenial—friendly

w.p.m.—words per minute, measures how fast a typist can type

call for appt—call for appointment, call to set time to come in

resume (pronounced REZ-oo-may)—a short description of your work experience and education

commission—in sales jobs, an amount you earn for each sale you make

salary commensurate with exp.—the more experience you have, the higher salary you will get

bi-lingual—can speak two languages

flexible hours—not just 9–5 pm, hours can change

QUESTIONS

**Look back at the ads on the last page.
Notice that each ad is numbered.**

1. Find 3 ads on the last page where typing is important. Check the numbers below.
   - ☐ Ad 1
   - ☐ Ad 2
   - ☐ Ad 3
   - ☐ Ad 4
   - ☐ Ad 5
   - ☐ Ad 6

2. Fred only types 45 words in one minute. Which job should he try for?
   - ☐ Ad 1
   - ☐ Ad 2
   - ☐ Ad 5

3. Which ad does not promise extras such as health insurance or paid vacations?
   - ☐ Ad 1
   - ☐ Ad 2
   - ☐ Ad 5

4. Which ad says there will be some freedom in choosing working hours?
   - ☐ Ad 3
   - ☐ Ad 4

5. Which person is bilingual?
   - ☐ Dan speaks English
   - ☐ Nidia speaks English and Spanish

6. What should you do if you are interested in the job in Ad 3?
   - ☐ call to set a time to go to the company
   - ☐ go to the company
   - ☐ send a resume to a box at the newspaper

7. What should you do if you are interested in the job in Ad 6?
   - ☐ call to set a time
   - ☐ go to the company
   - ☐ send a resume to a box at the newspaper

8. What does Ad 5 say about the office?
   - ☐ friendly
   - ☐ hard working

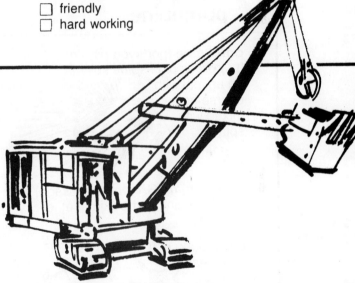

9. Louis has operated a crane for 6 months, Jay for 3 years. They both got jobs from Ad 3. Which is true?
   - ☐ Jay will get higher pay than Louis
   - ☐ They will both get the same pay

10. Which sales job sounds better for a person with no experience?
    - ☐ Ad 7
    - ☐ Ad 8

11. Which ad promises the salesman a percentage of every sale he makes in addition to his salary?
    - ☐ Ad 7
    - ☐ Ad 8

14. Using The Dictionary

Below is part of a page from a dictionary.

NOTICE

--the Guide Words at the top

--the alphabetical order of the words

--the kinds of information given about each word

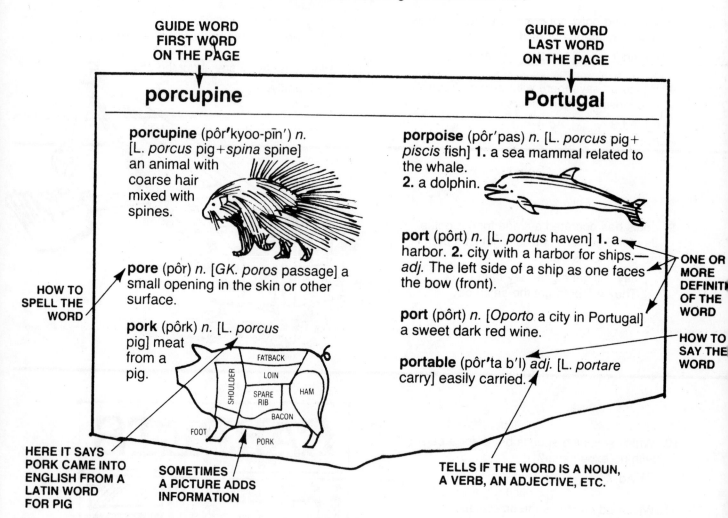

GUIDE WORD
FIRST WORD
ON THE PAGE

GUIDE WORD
LAST WORD
ON THE PAGE

porcupine

Portugal

porcupine (pôr′kyoo-pīn′) *n.* [L. *porcus* pig+*spina* spine] an animal with coarse hair mixed with spines.

pore (pôr) *n.* [*GK. poros* passage] a small opening in the skin or other surface.

pork (pôrk) *n.* [L. *porcus* pig] meat from a pig.

FATBACK
LOIN
SHOULDER
SPARE RIB
HAM
BACON
FOOT
PORK

porpoise (pôr′pas) *n.* [L. *porcus* pig+*piscis* fish] **1.** a sea mammal related to the whale. **2.** a dolphin.

port (pôrt) *n.* [L. *portus* haven] **1.** a harbor. **2.** city with a harbor for ships.—*adj.* The left side of a ship as one faces the bow (front).

port (pôrt) *n.* [*Oporto* a city in Portugal] a sweet dark red wine.

portable (pôr′ta b′l) *adj.* [L. *portare* carry] easily carried.

HOW TO
SPELL THE
WORD

HERE IT SAYS
PORK CAME INTO
ENGLISH FROM A
LATIN WORD
FOR PIG

SOMETIMES
A PICTURE ADDS
INFORMATION

TELLS IF THE WORD IS A NOUN,
A VERB, AN ADJECTIVE, ETC.

ONE OR
MORE
DEFINITI
OF THE
WORD

HOW TO
SAY THE
WORD

WORDS AND MEANINGS

Key to Pronunciation—the part of a dictionary that explains the special letters used in showing how a word is said aloud.

L—abbreviation for Latin, old language of the Roman Empire which has given many words to English

GK—abbreviation for Greek

QUESTIONS

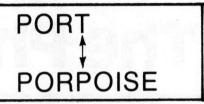

1. The words at the right begin with the same letters. The arrow shows the first letters that are different. Which letter comes first in the alphabet?

   ☐ P   ☐ T

2. Which word comes first in the dictionary?

   ☐ port   ☐ porpoise

A B C D E F G H I J K L M
N O P Q R S T U V W X Y Z

THE ALPHABET

3. Which page would have the word salamander on it?

   ☐ page 534
   ☐ page 535
   ☐ page 536

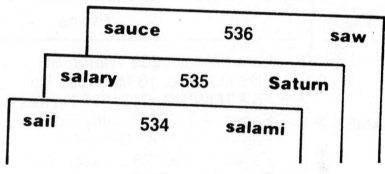

TOPS OF PAGES FROM A DICTIONARY

4. Look at the last page. Which comes first?

   ☐ port   ☐ portable

5. Which comes first in the dictionary?

   ☐ hubbub   ☐ hub

6. The Key to Pronunciation tells you to say ô just like the o in fork. Notice where it tells how to say porpoise. The por in porpoise should rhyme with

   ☐ car   ☐ door

7. Find the abbreviation that tells you porpoise is a <u>noun</u>. Circle it.

8. Look on the last page. Which word came from the Latin word for pig?

   ☐ porcupine   ☐ pore

9. On the last page there are many different definitions for port. Underline the only one that makes sense in this sentence:

   "The glass of port was a deep red color."

10. On the page opposite, circle the definition of <u>port</u> that makes the most sense in this sentence:

    "He stood on the <u>port</u> side of the ship."

15. Using The Phone Book

Below is a part of a page from a <u>Telephone Directory</u>, or phone book.

NOTICE

——the alphabetical order
——the Guide Words at the top

FIRST NAME ON PAGE   **LAST NAME ON PAGE**
▼   ▼

Evans   –   Fahey   95   ◄ **PAGE NUMBER**

NAMES ►

Ezra, Ronald, 259 Warren St.	755-2077
FBS Door Co. 16 Montrose Rd.	834-4424
F&Z TOWING, INC, 569 Haines Ave.	561-0344
Fagen, A.T. 330 Beverly Rd.	755-5323
Fagen, Arnold 42 Giles Rd.	832-7231
Fagen, Frank 473 Jackson Blvd	424-3220
Fagen, Mary 5 Wingate St	562-3876
Fahey, J.D. 75 24th Ave.	834-5421

◄ **TELEPHONE NUMBERS**

WORDS AND MEANINGS

digit—a single numeral. The number 43 has <u>2</u> digits

collect call—person <u>getting</u> call agrees to pay for it

area code—3-digit number you use for calls outside your local area. Dial the area code before the rest of the phone number. You may have to dial a 1 before the area code.

emergency—fire, sickness, crime, gas leak, any case needing fast help

QUESTIONS

Which comes first above?

1. ☐ A.T. Fagen   ☐ Arnold Fagen

Which comes first above?

2. ☐ Fagen, A.T.   ☐ F&Z Towing

3. Which should come first?

   ☐ H&L Co.   ☐ Harris, John

4. You want to call Alice Fagen. The phone may be in her husband's name. She lives on Jackson Boulevard. Which number should you try first?

5. Usually, but not always, businesses are listed by the <u>first</u> name. Where would you look for Eileen Gray's Bakery?

☐ B's ☐ E's ☐ G's

6. Numbers used as names are listed as if they were spelled out. <u>2 Oaks</u> is in the T's, as if it were spelled <u>Two Oaks</u>. What letter would you look under for <u>4-Star Construction Co.</u>?

☐ C ☐ F ☐ S

---

7. Abbreviations are listed as if they were spelled out. On which page at the right would you find <u>St. Louis Restaurant</u>?

☐ page 75 ☐ page 77

	PAGE
SNYDER–TAYLOR	77
RYAN–SMILEY	75

---

8. Look at the Index at the right. On what page would you look for a number to call if you wanted to report a fire?

_____

9. You want to call a friend in another state and have him pay for the call. On what page should you look for directions?

_____

TELEPHONE DIRECTORY INDEX

	PAGE
EMERGENCY NUMBERS	inside back cover
Area Codes and Maps	6–7
Area served by this directory	outside back cover
Bill payment	5
Business office	5
Instructions for dialing calls	
Collect	3
Credit card	3
Direct dialed	4
Overseas	4

---

10. You want to call 431-2741 in San Antonio, Texas, from Chicago. At the right is an area code map of Texas. Find the area code for San Antonio. Then write the complete phone number just the way you would dial it.

_____

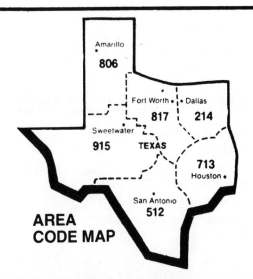

AREA CODE MAP

16. Using The Yellow Pages

The Yellow Pages help you find the business that sells what you want to buy or does what you want done.

Below is a part of a page from the Yellow Pages.
NOTICE that the main headings are kinds of business and that they are in alphabetical order.

PAVING–PET

HARVEY'S BLACK TOP AND PAVING CO.
47 WEST ST.

- PARKING LOTS
- TENNIS COURTS
- PLAYGROUNDS

752-4700   FREE ESTIMATES

WAVERLY PRODUCTS, INC.
ROAD BUILDING
541-7831
7400 Richmond Hwy.

NOAH'S ARK
- AKC PUPPIES
- BIRDS
- TROPICAL FISH

733-5321
51 BROADWAY

CREDIT TERMS

▶**PAVING CONTRACTORS**

HARVEY'S BLACKTOP & PAVING CO.
 See our ad this page
 47 West St   752-4700
NORTH-STAR PAVING
 Blacktop, Driveways, Lots,
 Tennis Courts, No Job Too Small
 1666 Orton Ave   831-3441
WAVERLY PRODUCTS, INC
 See our ad this page
 7400 Richmond Hwy   541-7831

▶**PEST CONTROL**
 See Exterminating

▶**PET SHOPS**
NOAH'S ARK
 See our ad this page
 51 Broadway   733-5321

▶**PET SUPLS & FOODS–RETAIL**
ROMA PET SUPPLIES
 Everything for your pet
 4720 Patchin Terrace   831-4241

▶**PET SUPLS & FOODS–WHOL.**
ARLO PET SUPPLIES, INC
 432 E. Fenton   733-4220

WORDS AND MEANINGS

supls—supplies, things needed like paint or nails or paper

contractor—someone who agrees to organize and supervise a job. The contractor brings in the workers and supplies

dlrs—dealers, companies selling things

estimate—amount of money the contractor thinks the job will cost you.

whol—wholesale, sells items only to other businesses, usually in large amounts, usually cheaper than you can buy them

retail—sells to anyone. The stores you buy at are retail stores.

exterminating—getting rid of bugs or mice

QUESTIONS

1. This mark ▶ points to:
- [ ] company names
- [ ] kinds of businesses

2. You want to buy dog collars to sell in your pet store. Which number should you call?
- [ ] 831-4241
- [ ] 733-4220

3. Liz wants to get rid of her roaches. She looked up Insect but found nothing. Then she looked up Pest Control.

Look at the page opposite. What should she do next?
- [ ] give up
- [ ] call the number
- [ ] turn to the E's

4. You want to blacktop an empty lot for a basketball court. Look under Paving Contractors. Read the listing for the 3 companies. Look for any ads and read them.

You want to have someone come look at the job, add up all the costs, and tell you about what you will have to pay. Which company says they will do this for free?
- [ ] Harvey's
- [ ] North-Star

5. Which company seems more interested in paving roads than playgrounds and courts?
- [ ] Harvey's
- [ ] North-Star
- [ ] Waverly

6. You want someone to paint your store. What should you look under?
- [ ] Paint—Retail
- [ ] Paint—Whol.
- [ ] Painting Contractors

7. You want to buy a new table for your apartment. Which should you look for in the Yellow Pages?
- [ ] Furniture—Retail
- [ ] Furniture—Whol.

8. Below are the tops of 2 pages from the Yellow Pages. Look at the Guide Words at the top. On which page would you look for furniture?
- [ ] p. 93
- [ ] p. 94

P 94 FURNACES – GAMES

FROZEN – FUR   P 93

17. Reading Timetables

Below is a timetable for the Panama Limited. This train goes from Chicago to New Orleans and New Orleans to Chicago. The timetable lists all the places where the train stops and the times.

NOTICE how many abbreviations and symbols are used. These are explained under **Reference Marks**.

The Panama Limited	Chicago Champaign Carbondale Memphis Jackson New Orleans		Transtrak Train Timetable Effective October 29, 1985	Chicago-Texas/ Louisiana

READ DOWN				READ UP		
59		Train Number			**58**	
Daily		Frequency of Operation			Daily	
Ⓡ 🛏 ✕ 🖻		Type of Service			Ⓡ 🛏 ✕ 🖻	
		(Illinois Central Gulf)				
4 20P	Dp	Chicago, IL *(Union Sta.) (CT)*		Ar	10 45A	
⊗ 5 02P		Homewood, IL		D	9 45A	
5 32P		Kankakee, IL			9 04A	
6 22P		Rantoul, IL			8 12A	
6 50P		Champaign-Urbana, IL			7 56A	
7 32P		Mattoon, IL			6 57A	
7 59P		Effingham, IL ⊕			6 31A	
9 00P		Centralia, IL ⊕			5 46A	
9 50P 10 05P	Ar Dp	Carbondale, IL 🚌 *(St. Louis)*		Dp Ar	4 50A 4 35A	
11 13P		Cairo, IL ●			3 29A	
12 15A		Fulton, KY ●			2 32A	
1 07A		Dyersburg, TN ●			1 32A	
2 50A 3 05A	Ar Dp	Memphis, TN		Dp Ar	11 55P 11 40P	
4 17A		Batesville, MS ●			10 22P	
5 05A		Grenada, MS ●			9 36P	
5 28A		Winona, MS ●			9 16P	
5 59A		Durant, MS			8 48P	
6 35A		Canton, MS ●			8 16P	
7 08A		Jackson, MS			7 43P	
F 7 39A		Hazlehurst, MS ● ∅		F	7 04P	
8 01A		Brookhaven, MS ●			6 43P	
8 31A		McComb, MS ●			6 21P	
9 22A		Hammond, LA			5 30P	
10 35A	Ar	New Orleans, LA *(CT)*		Dp	4 30P	

Transtrak

Reference Marks

Ⓡ All reserved train.

🛏 Sleeping car service.

✕ Complete dining and beverage service.

⊠ Tray meal and beverage service.

🖻 Checked baggage handled. Consult agent or services listing for exceptions.

🚌 Via direct motor coach.

● Tickets not available at station. Purchase tickets on train.

⊕ Ticket office not open at all train departure times. When ticket office is closed fare may be paid on train without penalty.

∅ Experimental stop for trial period. Stop may be discontinued if usage does not justify continuation.

D Stops only to discharge passengers.

F Stops only on signal to receive or discharge passengers, where possible, please give sufficient advance notice to agent or conductor.

⊗ Passengers not carried locally between this station and Chicago except when connecting at Chicago to or from other trains.

⊕ Transfer service provided from station, 1174 East Commerce St., 30 minutes prior to departure of trains 21 and 22.

A -A.M.   P -P.M.   (CT) -Central time.

Km -Kilometers.   Mi -Miles.

WORDS AND MEANINGS

stops only to discharge passengers— people can get off but not on

all-reserved train—no one can ride the train without a reservation

motor coach—a bus. Passengers to some cities may have to get off the train and change to a motor coach

reservation—an agreement that the train company will save a place on the train for the customer. You must notify the train company ahead of time. You must say where you are coming from, where you are going to, and the date and time

QUESTIONS

1. Look at the times in the column headed READ DOWN. They are for people who are going from Chicago to a station further down the timetable.

   When should you look under READ DOWN?
   - [ ] when you are going from Chicago to New Orleans
   - [ ] when you are going from New Orleans to Chicago

2. You are in Jackson, MS. You want to go to Memphis, TN. Which column do you look in for train times?
   - [ ] READ DOWN
   - [ ] READ UP

3. What time does the train leave Jackson for Memphis?
   - [ ] 7 08A
   - [ ] 7 43P

4. On the timetable, the time 9 07A would mean 7 minutes past 9 in the morning. The A stands for AM—the hours from midnight to noon. P after a time means PM—the hours from noon to midnight.

   When does the train leave Jackson for Memphis?
   - [ ] morning
   - [ ] evening

5. **AR** means arrives—the time a train pulls into a station.

   DP means departs—the time a train leaves a station.

   When does the train to Chicago leave Memphis?
   - [ ] 2 50A
   - [ ] 3 05A
   - [ ] 11 55P
   - [ ] 11 40P

6. When does the train from Chicago pull into Carbondale?
   - [ ] 9 50P
   - [ ] 10 05P
   - [ ] 4 50A
   - [ ] 4 35A

7. Look up the symbol to the right of Carbondale, IL. Find the symbol in the Reference Marks list. Then go to the WORDS AND MEANINGS.

   How does a passenger to Carbondale get to St. Louis?
   - [ ] continues on the train
   - [ ] takes another train
   - [ ] takes a bus

8. You want to go from Homewood (just below Chicago) to Chicago. Notice the **D** next to the time. Look it up in the Reference Marks list. What does it mean?
   - [ ] you can't use this train
   - [ ] the train departs at 9 45 in the morning

9. Look in the first and last columns next to the heading Type of Service. Notice the symbol $\boxed{R}$. What does it tell you about the train?
   - [ ] it runs daily in both directions
   - [ ] you can't take it unless you reserve a seat ahead of time

10. You are traveling from Chicago to Hazlehurst, MS, just below Jackson, MS. Look carefully at all the symbols on the Hazlehurst line of the timetable. What should you do? (Check more than one)
    - [ ] check beforehand to see if the train still makes stops there
    - [ ] take a different train—this one doesn't stop at Hazleburst
    - [ ] notify the conductor ahead of time so the train can make a special stop at Hazlehurst
    - [ ] do nothing special

11. You're traveling from Cairo, IL (just below Carbondale, IL) to New Orleans. Where must you buy your ticket?
    - [ ] at the station only
    - [ ] on the train only
    - [ ] either train or station

12. Look at the symbols at the right. Which symbol would you look for if you wanted your meals brought to you on a tray?
    - [ ] A
    - [ ] B
    - [ ] C
    - [ ] D

A   B   C   D

18. Reading Street Maps

Below is part of a street map of the town of Pascagoula, Mississippi.

NOTICE the letters and numbers on the top and side margins.

NOTICE the small numbers in circles on the map itself. The lesson will tell you what they mean.

NOTICE the arrow pointing NORTH.

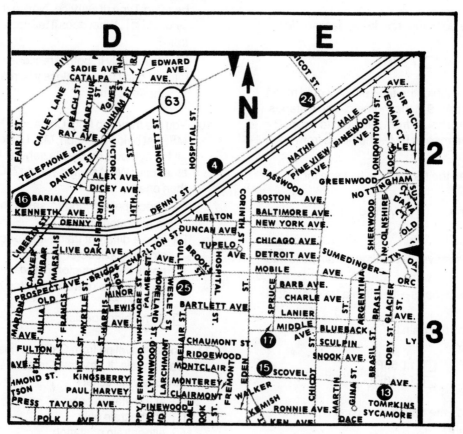

1. Street maps usually have a section labeled "Street Index." It tells you how to find the different streets or avenues that are on the map.

   Street maps may also have a section labeled "Points of Interest." This section tells you how to find schools, banks, shopping centers, and other important buildings or places.

   Where would you look to find each of the following?

   Mobile Avenue
   ☐ Street Index   ☐ Points of Interest

   City Hall
   ☐ Street Index   ☐ Points of Interest

   Cherokee School
   ☐ Street Index   ☐ Points of Interest

   Library
   ☐ Street Index   ☐ Points of Interest

   Potomac Drive
   ☐ Street Index   ☐ Points of Interest

2. Maps are often divided into squares like the box at the right. Each square on the box can be named by a combination of the letter above and the number at the side.

What is the name of the shaded square?

☐ B1   ☐ B3   ☐ C3

3. Sometimes the lines dividing the map into squares are not actually drawn. But you can see where they would go from clues on the outside border of the map.

Look at the box on the right. What square is the dot in?

☐ A2   ☐ A3   ☐ B2   ☐ C1

4. At the right is part of the Street Index for Pascagoula. It lists streets in alphabetical order. Where on the map would you look for Snook Avenue?

☐ D2   ☐ D3   ☐ E2   ☐ E3

SINGING RIVER ST. D,E4	SOUTHSHORE AVE. E5
SIR RICHARD AVE. E,F2	SOUTHWOOD AVE. D,E5
SKIP AVE C3	SPANISH AVE. C2
SMALL AVE. E4	SPRUCE ST. C3
SMITH AVE. D4	SUFFOLK ST. F2
SNOOK AVE. E3	SUMEDINGER ST. E3

5. Find Snook Avenue on the map and draw a line around it like this:

(SNOOK AVE)

6. Find the Singing River Hospital in the Points of Interest at the right. What is the number inside the black dot before the hospital's name?

7. Where is the hospital on the map?

☐ D2   ☐ D3   ☐ E2   ☐ E3

8. On the map, find the numbered black dot that shows where the Singing River Hospital is. Draw a circle around it.

POINTS OF INTEREST

❶ CHAMBER OF COMMERCE C2
❷ CITY HALL C3
❸ COURT HOUSE C3
❹ SINGING RIVER HOSPITAL D2
❺ LIBRARY C3
❻ POST OFFICE C3
❼ BEACH PARK & PUBLIC BEACH
   RECREATION AREA D5

9. You are on the corner of Snook Ave. and Chicot St. You want to go to Singing River Hospital. You must follow these directions:

"Go north along Chicot St. to Mobile Ave. Turn left on Mobile and go to Hospital St. Turn right on Hospital and continue under the railroad tracks to Denny St. Turn right on Denny and go a short distance to the hospital on your left."

Draw your route on the map. Start at the corner of Snook and Chicot and finish at the hospital.

Unit 3 Review

1. Whose name would probably be listed first in a telephone book?
   - ☐ C. H. Moon
   - ☐ Carla Moon

2. You want to look up the phone number of the Abigail Adams Smith Museum in the phone book. Where should you look first?
   - ☐ under the A's
   - ☐ under the S's
   - ☐ under the M's

3. You wish to find a florist in the Yellow Pages who will send flowers by telegram. What do you look under?
   - ☐ Florists, Retail
   - ☐ Florists, Whol.
   - ☐ Retail Florists
   - ☐ Whol. Florists

4. Which of the following is usually in alphabetical order?
   - ☐ Index
   - ☐ Table of Contents

5. Which of the following words comes first in a dictionary?
   - ☐ log
   - ☐ loganberry
   - ☐ loft

6. The tops of 3 pages in a dictionary look like this:

mill	538	mi
minded	539	minor
minor	540	misbeliever

   On what page would you find the word **mining**?
   - ☐ 538   ☐ 539   ☐ 540

7. Look at the TV schedule. How many shows at 8:00 appear to be re-runs?
   - ☐ 1   ☐ 2   ☐ more than 2

8. What time does the Yankees–Brewers ball game start?
   - ☐ 8:00   ☐ 8:30   ☐ 9:00

9. Who is Carol Burnett's guest at 11:00?
   - ☐ Roddy McDowall
   - ☐ Benny Hill
   - ☐ Dick Cavett

10. A new show called The Runaways starts at 8:00. How long does it last?
    - ☐ 1/2 hour   ☐ 1 hour   ☐ 2 hours

TUESDAY EVENING PROGRAMS

8:00 ❷ WONDER WOMAN — Unaware that her secret identity has been discovered, Diana continues her investigation of an invasion of "mind-snatchers." Part 2.
❹ THE RUNAWAYS — (Season Premiere). Alan Feinstein stars as a pyschologist hired to rescue two high school girls from a work farm run by a corrupt sheriff.
❺ THE CROSS WITS
❼ HAPPY DAYS — Fonzie creates a new dance craze. (R)
❾ AMERICAN LIFE STYLE — "Benjamin Franklin."
⓫ CELEBRITY CHARADES
⓭ SPECIAL EDITION
8:30 ❺ MERV GRIFFIN — Dean-Paul Martin, producer Robert Evans, Marilyn Sokol, British comedian Bruce Forsyth, Minnie Ripperton.
❼ LAVERNE AND SHIRLEY — Laverne, backed by managers Lenny and Squiggy and dance coach Carmine, travels to Chicago to audition for a role in "West Side Story." (R)
❾ BASEBALL — Mets at St. Louis.
⓫ BASEBALL — Yankees at Milwaukee Brewers.

⓭ SKYLINE — "The Kings of Flatbush." Nostalgic film portrait of the Kings Theater movie palace.
9:00 ❷ MOVIE — "The Survival of Dana."
❹ MOVIE — "The Revengers."
❼ THREE'S COMPANY — Roper plays such a dirty trick to keep the roommates from having a party that Helen leaves him. (R)
⓭ AN APPLE, AN ORANGE — Chronicle of the sensitive relationship between two immigrant women, one Dutch, the other Chinese.
9:30 ❼ TAXI — As Latka hurries to repair Cab 804, the cabbies continue to reminsce about it. Part 2. (R)
10:00 ❺ NEWS, WEATHHER, SPORTS
❼ THE BARBARA WALTERS SPECIAL — George Burns, Mary Tyler Moore, Penny Marshall and Rob Reiner and Richard Pryor.
10:30 ⓭ RUN AMERICA RUN — A look at this country's mania for running.
11:00 ❷❹❼⓫ NEWS, WEATHER, SPORTS
❺ CAROL BURNETT — Roddy McDowall.
❾ BENNY HILL
⓭ DICK CAVETT

11. The "Points of Interest" key to this map says that the Mt. Hebron School is in Square **C11**. Find it and draw a circle around it.

12. Look at the Street Index below. Where is Club Road?

  ☐ **B11**   ☐ **C11**   ☐ **D11**

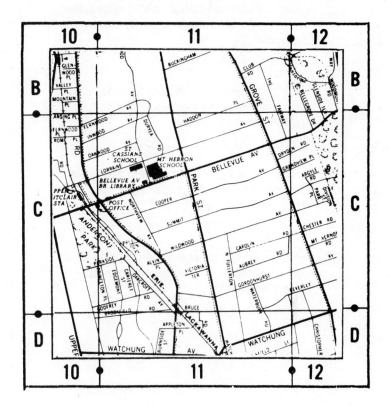

Claremont Av. E11	Club Rd. B11
Claremont Pl. E12	Club St. D11
Clarewill Av. B11	College Av. A10
Cleveland Rd. D12	Columbus Av. D12
Clinton Av. F11	Cooper Av. C11
Cloverhill Pl. E12	Cornell Way B12

13. Find the corner of Club Road and Grove Street on the map and mark it with an **X**.

14. To get to Mt. Hebron School from the corner of Club and Grove, you drive south along Grove until you come to Bellevue Ave. Turn west on Bellevue until you cross Park St. Continue to the school.

   Starting at the spot you marked with an X, draw a heavy line on the map to show the route you would take to the school.

---

15. Millie Hawkins is interested in an auto polisher's job, but she has no job experience. She does have a clean driver's license. Which newspaper ad should she answer?

   ☐ Ad 1   ☐ Ad 2   ☐ neither

16. Vic Sandoval is interested in an auto polisher's job. He has 1 year's experience. His driver's license has been suspended for 6 months. Which newspaper ad should he answer?

   ☐ Ad 1   ☐ Ad 2   ☐ neither

17. Carmen Reyes speaks Spanish and English. She is looking for a full-time clerk typist job. Which ad looks better to her?

   ☐ Ad 3   ☐ Ad 4   ☐ neither

18. Nick Yiannis wants a part time clerk typist's job in the afternoon, after school. Which ad looks better for him?

   ☐ Ad 3   ☐ Ad 4   ☐ neither

51

19. Ellie Mikulski hopes to find a 4- or 5- room apartment with wall-to-wall carpeting already installed. Which ad would probably interest her most?

☐ Ad 3   ☐ Ad 5   ☐ Ad 6

20. Julius and Lois McDaniel have a child and a dog. Which apartment ad would probably be best for them to look into?

☐ Ad 1   ☐ Ad 2   ☐ Ad 3

21. Bud Schultze wants an apartment that's near a bus or train line. Which apartment looks like it might meet this need?

☐ Ad 3   ☐ Ad 4   ☐ Ad 5

22. Nina Jensen is a college student looking for a room off campus. Which ad would probably interest her most?

☐ Ad 1   ☐ Ad 2   ☐ Ad 5

23. What time does the train leave Boise, ID, for Salt Lake City, UT?

_____ (write the hour)

in the ☐ morning   ☐ evening (check one)

24. Do you need to have a reservation to ride on this train? (Look back at the Reference Marks on page 46 if you need to.)

☐ yes   ☐ no

READ DOWN				READ UP
25		Train Number		26
Daily		Frequency of Operation		Daily
🛏 ☒ ☐		Type of Service		🛏 ☒ ☐
		(Union Pacific)		
11 25 P	Dp	**Salt Lake City, UT** *(Amtrak Sta.) (MT)* Ar		7 10 A
12 20 A	Ar	**Ogden, UT**	Dp	6 10 A
12 35 A	Dp		Ar	5 55 A
F 1 05 A		Brigham City, UT ●		F 5 25 A
3 20 A	Ar	**Pocatello, ID**	Dp	3 10 A
3 30 A	Dp		Ar	3 00 A
5 15 A		Shoshone, ID ●		1 10 A
F 6 30 A		Mountain Home, ID ●		F 11 55 P
7 30 A		**Boise, ID**		10 50 P

Unit IV.
PAY, BILLS, AND TAXES

Life Skills Reading is more than just reading words. It's reading numbers, too. The numbers on your paycheck, on a credit card, on a utility bill, on a check, on your bank records, on a tax form.

Are you being paid the right amount? Learn how to read your paycheck stub so you'll know.

If you always pay the amount a bill asks for, you may be overpaying. Read the whole bill, and you could save money.

Reading about your own money is a skill that helps you watch out for yourself.

CONTENTS OF THIS UNIT

19. Reading Utility Bills

Below is a Telephone Bill.

READ Line 1, the regular <u>Monthly Charge</u>.

NOTICE all the other charges. You should always read bills before paying them.

——The company can make mistakes

——So can you (letting a friend call across the country)

New York Telephone

your telephone number
212 850 5587   061

Date of this bill   JAN 7 85

| | 0305 | 0308 | U | 4M |

Please return the enclosed card with your payment

When paying in person, please bring your bill and the card.

FRANK CARUSO
PO BOX 300 RED HOOK STA
BROOKLYN NY   11231

	State-Local Tax	Federal Tax	Charges Excluding Taxes
1 Monthly Charge for Service	64	24	8 00
2 Local Usage (see Statement)	03	01	37
3 Directory Assistance and Toll Calls (see Statement)	12	26	8 57
4 Other Charges or Credits (see explanation)			
5 Representation in Directory (explanation enclosed)			
6 Total of Current Charges Excluding Taxes			16 94
7 Taxes	79	51	1 30
8 Total of Current Charges Including Taxes			18 24
9 Balance from Last Bill (please disregard this amount if paid)			10 00
		Total ➝	28 24

If you have a question or complaint call our Business Office ➝ 212 624 9950

Please pay by ▶   FEB 1   Thank you

WORDS AND MEANINGS

utility—useful service like electricity, gas, telephone

local usage—calls to nearby area. You may be charged for local calls after the first 30 or 40 or so.

toll calls—long distance, calls outside the local area. You get charged for the time you talk.

directory assistance—when the operator tells you someone's phone number

balance—amount of money

disregard—don't do anything

current charges—amount from this bill, not the last one.

complaint—telling what's wrong

QUESTIONS

1. Which line on the phone bill is for calls to nearby places?

   ☐ Line 2   ☐ Line 3

2. What are the charges for calling long distance and for asking for telephone numbers?

   ☐ 37¢   ☐ $8.57

3. Below is another page from the same bill. This page explains the $8.57 on Line 3. On what date did someone call Alexandria, Virginia?

   ☐ Dec. 14   ☐ Dec. 20   ☐ Dec. 29

4. How long did someone talk to St. Helena, California on December 20th? (Look under Min. for minutes)

   ☐ 3 min.   ☐ 14 min.   ☐ 26 min.

Statement of Charges and Credits for Calls

Page	Billing Number 850 5587	Calling Number 850 5587			1-7900
2		2			
Date			Amount	Min.	Hr. Min. C
	TOLL CALLS				
1212	ST HELENA CA	707 963 2485	52	3	2 33 82
1214	ALEXANDRIA VA	703 550 9475	169	14	2 33 92
1220	ST HELENA CA	707 963 2485	401	26	2 35 62
1229	WARWICK NY	914 986 5130	59	1	09 35 0
1231	HYATTSVL MD	301 927 8931	147	13	1 61 72
1231	ANNAPOLIS MD	301 757 3615	29	2	1 62 22
TOTAL TOLL			857		

5. What is Line 8 on the phone bill on the opposite page?

   ☐ amount owed from before
   ☐ new charges

6. What is Line 9?

   ☐ amount owed from before
   ☐ new charges

7. If Frank never paid the amount on Line 9, what should he pay now?

   ☐ $18.24   ☐ $28.24

8. If Frank sent the $10.00 in a few days ago, what should he pay now?

   ☐ $18.24   ☐ $28.24

9. If Frank sent the $10.00 in a month ago, something must be wrong. What number should he call to ask about it?

10. Which is not a utility bill?

    ☐ electricity   ☐ rent
    ☐ gas   ☐ telephone

20. Paying Bills By Check

Below is a check made out to the gas company.
NOTICE how each line is filled out.

FRANK CARUSO   N̲o̲.   310

Dec 16 19 84   1·8/210
Branch 123

PAY TO THE ORDER OF ___Brooklyn Union Gas___ $ 13 50

___Thirteen and 50/100___ ∿∿∿ DOLLARS

First National Bank

FOR ___gas bill AccT 1620/53214___   _Frank Caruso_

⑈021000089⑈ 123 231749727⑈ 0310

WORDS AND MEANINGS

Pay to the order of—on a check, the bank will pay the person or company on this line

Previous balance—on a bill, amount owed before this bill came out

Account number—number given to each customer by a company. Each one is different

credited to your account—subtracted from what you owed

QUESTIONS

1. Find the date JAN. 15, 1985 at the bottom of the electric bill on the next page. Read the 2 lines above it. You sent them a check for $8.20 on Jan. 16. Has the company had time to subtract $8.20 from what you owe?

   ☐ yes   ☐ no

2. Read the Previous balance and the Current charges on the right-hand side of the bill. You already sent the $8.20. How much do you owe now?

   ☐ $8.20   ☐ $9.19   ☐ $17.39

3. Today's date is January 20, 1985. Write this date on the blank check on the next page. Use the check above as an example.

4. The name of the electric company is Tri-State Edison. Write this in the blank that shows who should get the money.

5. Write the amount of money you owe (from Question 2) on the blank next to the $ sign. Use numbers, not words.

6. On the blank next to the word DOLLARS write out the amount of money in words for the dollars and in fraction numbers for the cents. Look back at the example to see how.

7. Write electric bill in the blank next to the FOR on the check.

8. Find the Account number on the bill. Copy this number also on the line on the check next to FOR. Label it Acct. No. This will help the company credit your account, not someone else's.

9. Sign the check with your name.

10. Look over the whole check.
--Are all the blanks filled in?
--Is everything correct?
--Is it easy to read?
Fix anything that is wrong.

TRI-STATE Edison

Account number	For information call	Next meter reading	Previous balance
61 1368 102 1 0006 4	212-624-6300	FEB 15	8 20

83

Service period From Month Day To Month Day Year	Number of days	Service class	Meter readings Previous	Code	Present	Code	Meter multiplier	Usage Kwh. or 100 Cu. ft.	Current charges
12 15 1 16 79	32	EL 1	1161	A	1168	A	10	70	9 19

Service address	Demand in kilowatts	Sales tax included in bill
177 COLUMBIA ST 2 FL		60

Fuel and gas adjustments factor	amount	Transfer adjustment factor	amount	Payments received through this date have been credited to your account.	
Electric Gas .0751	05			JAN 15 1985	17 39

127

1-1/210 61

_____ 19____

PAY
TO THE
ORDER OF _____ $ _____

_____ DOLLARS

First National Bank

FOR_____   _____

⑁⑆:0 2 10000 18⑆:   ⑉47 4681⑉ 0127

21. Paying with Money Orders

The Post Office sells Money Orders. They are safe and easy to use when you want to send money to someone or pay for things you order by mail. It costs more to use Money Orders than checks, but you don't need a bank account to buy them.

NOTICE below, that the <u>Post Office</u> stamps the Money Order with the exact amount you ask for.

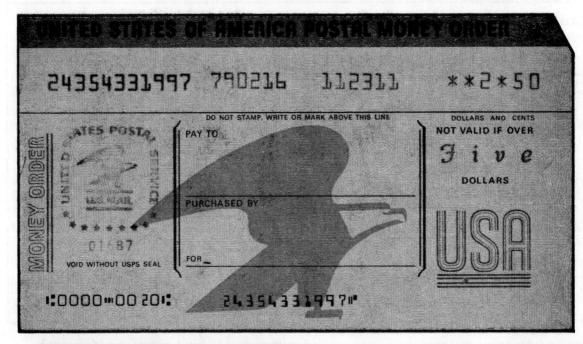

WORDS AND MEANINGS

provided you fill in—only if you fill in

receipt—a piece of paper that shows you paid for something

present this receipt—show this receipt

not negotiable—cannot be used like money

void—no good

not valid—no good

making a claim—asking for your money back

endorse—sign one's name on the back of a check or Money Order. The person who <u>receives</u> a Money Order must endorse it before the Post Office will cash it.

QUESTIONS

1. When you buy a Money Order, what does the <u>Post Office</u> fill in?
   - ☐ the amount
   - ☐ the name of the person that the Money Order will be paid to

2. What do <u>you</u> fill in?
   - ☐ the amount
   - ☐ the name of the person that the Money Order will be paid to

3. As soon as you buy a Money Order, fill it out with the name of the person or company you are paying. The one on the last page is for a book from the T.J. Schwab mail order catalog. Write "T.J. Schwab" in the **PAY TO** space of the Money Order on the page opposite.

4. Put your own name in the **PURCHASED BY** space.

5. Write "Book" in the **FOR** space.

6. Before sending a Money Order, rip the **Customer's Receipt** off the top and save it. Can you buy anything with the receipt shown below? (Look at it carefully.)

   ☐ yes   ☐ no

7. Suppose the Money Order is lost. What must you do before you can get your money back? (Read the instructions on the bottom of the Customer's Receipt.)

   ☐ prove that the loss wasn't your fault
   ☐ wait 60 days before making the claim

8. If the Money Order is lost or stolen and you want a refund, what should you do with the receipt?

   ☐ bring it to the Post Office
   ☐ mail it to the person in the **PAY TO** space

9. When you buy a Money Order, you pay an additional charge for the Post Office's services. What is the total amount you would pay for a Money Order for $10?

   ☐ $10   ☐ more than $10

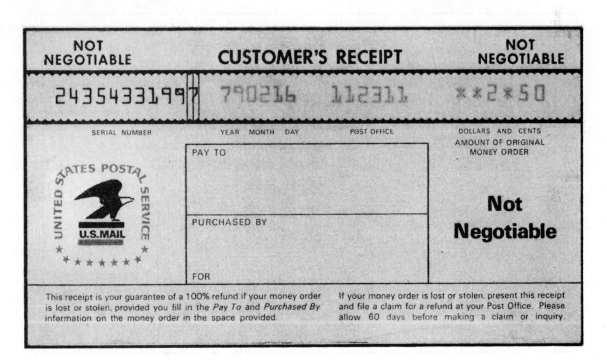

10. Robyn Lucas was sent a Money Order in the mail. Her name was in the **PAY TO** space on the front. She cashed it at the Post Office. To do this, she showed her driver's license as identification and signed the back of the Money Order. Where did she sign?

    ☐ where it says **PAY TO**
    ☐ where it says **ENDORSEMENT**

PAY TO: (Person or firm)

ENDORSEMENT: (Signature, address, identification)

BACK OF A MONEY ORDER

22. Bank Statements

Rosa Gonzales has a checking account with her local bank. Every month the bank sends her back the checks she wrote that they have received and processed. The bank also sends her a bank statement. This is a record of all the money that went into and out of her account that month.

LOOK at Rosa's bank statement below.

NOTICE the column headings and how each item is listed in the statement.

If you don't understand the meaning of a word on the statement, look it up in the WORDS AND MEANINGS.

STATEMENT OF ACCOUNT

First National Bank

ROSA GONZALES
12 OLD SPANISH TRAIL
HOUSTON TX 77021

PO BOX 43
MAIN POST OFFICE
HOUSTON, TEXAS

For Inquiries
Please Call 873-2700

ACCOUNT NO. 23131742

CHECK NO. OR DESCRIPTION	DEBITS	CREDITS	DATE	BALANCE
OPENING BALANCE			10/01	196.67
234	150.00		10/11	46.67
DEPOSIT		220.00	10/18	266.67
236	50.00		10/24	216.67
237	75.50		10/27	141.17
238	8.77		10/28	132.40
DEPOSIT		230.00	10/29	362.40
SERVICE CHARGE	1.40		10/30	361.00
CLOSING BALANCE			10/30	361.00
TOTAL DEBITS	285.67			
TOTAL CREDITS		450.00		
TOTAL SERVICE CHARGES	1.40			

WORDS AND MEANINGS

debit—the bank's record of money going out of your account. In a statement, the bank lists checks in the debits column

credit—the bank's record of money going into your account. In a statement, the bank lists your deposits in the credits column

balance—the amount of money in your account. Your bank balance changes every time you write a check or make a deposit

opening balance—your balance at the beginning of the month covered by the statement

deposit—money you put into a bank account

service charge—money the bank charges you for handling your checking account. The bank takes the service charge directly from your account every month, and lists it in the debits column of your statement.

closing balance—your balance at the end of the month

QUESTIONS

1. Look at the statement. How much money did Rosa have in the bank at the beginning of the month?

$ _____

2. How much money did she have in the bank at the end of the month?

$ _____

3. Rosa paid her rent with a check. LOOK at the check and at the statement. When was the money for this check taken out of her account?

☐ Oct. 5
☐ Oct. 11
☐ Oct. 30

4. Look at the deposit ticket Rosa filled out.

Find where this deposit is listed on the statement. Circle the word DEPOSIT, the date, and the amount.

5. Look back at the bank statement. How much did the bank charge for handling Rosa's account?

$ _____

6. On October 13, Rosa deposited $220 in checks. It took a short time for the bank to actually collect the money and put it in Rosa's account.

Look at the statement. When did the money go into Rosa's account?

☐ 10-11
☐ 10-18
☐ 10-29

7. Rosa once wrote a check for more money than there was in her account. The check was no good. This caused the bank some trouble, and they charged her $4.00.

Where would the bank have listed the $4.00 on the statement?

☐ in the debits column
☐ in the credits column
☐ in the balance column

CHECK NUMBER 234	First National Bank	50.254 213
	DATE Oct 5 19 85	
PAY TO THE ORDER OF Victor Valdez	.150 %/00	
One hundred fifty and ⁰⁰/₁₀₀	DOLLARS	
⑆0213⹀231317⒋2	Rosa Gonzalez	

Deposit Checking — First National Bank

Date 10-29-85		Dollars	Cents
	Cash	230	00
Account at (if other than this branch) —	Checks 1		
Full Title of Account	List Separately 2		
Rosa Gonzalez	3		
	4		
Address 12 Old Spanish 7	5		
Houston Tx 77021	6		
	7		
Account Number 2 3 1 3 1	Total	230	00

8. Look at the statement. What is the date of the closing balance?

☐ 10-29
☐ 10-30
☐ not dated

9. On 10-31, Rosa wrote a check for $20. Where is the check listed on this statement?

☐ in the credits column
☐ at the bottom
☐ It isn't listed. It will be listed in next month's statement

23. Charge Account Statements

If you have a charge account or a credit card, or if you are buying something on time, you'll get a statement of your account every month.

The statement will tell you what you owed last month. It will bring you up to date on what you charged and what you owe this month. And it will tell you how much money you must send in before the next statement comes out.

LOOK carefully at the statement below.

NOTICE the one purchase that Steve Lambrakis made. And **NOTICE** how it affected his statement.

SUPER-CHARGE

Statement Date
APRIL 4, 1985

Account Number
4372 4171

PLEASE PAY BY NEXT BILLING DATE
MAY 4, 1985

STEVE LAMBRAKIS
18 EAST WILLIAM STREET
BENTON IL 62812

DATE	PURCHASE	REFERENCE NUMBER	AMOUNT
03/15/85	ELECTRONIC GAME	A-473-241	100.00

PREVIOUS BALANCE	PURCHASES	PAYMENTS	FINANCE CHARGE	NEW BALANCE	MINIMUM PAYMENT DUE
200.00	100.00	10.00	3.00	293.00	12.00

WORDS AND MEANINGS

previous balance—the total amount owed on last month's statement

purchases—the total amount bought with the charge card since the last statement

payments—all payments that were received by the charge card company after the last statement came out

finance charge—money that you pay for using a charge account to buy things. It's a percentage of the unpaid balance. (Often there's no finance charge on this month's purchases. And there won't be one till next month's.)

new balance—the new total amount owed at the time the statement was made out

creditor—someone you owe money to. It's not always the place where you bought something. In this case, it's the company that sends you the statement

QUESTIONS

1. Look at the top of the April statement on the last page.

   When should Steve send his payment in?
   - [ ] by April 4
   - [ ] by May 4
   - [ ] by June 4

2. When did Steve make his last purchase?
   - [ ] March 15
   - [ ] April 4
   - [ ] May 4

3. How much did Steve charge with his Super-Charge card since the last billing date?
   - [ ] $200
   - [ ] $100
   - [ ] can't tell from the statement

4. How much did Steve send in as his last payment?
   - [ ] $10
   - [ ] $3
   - [ ] $12
   - [ ] can't tell from the statement

5. What's the smallest amount that Steve must send in this month?
   - [ ] $10
   - [ ] $3
   - [ ] $12
   - [ ] can't tell from the statement

6. Suppose Steve sends in the minimum payment due. What's the total amount that he will owe then?
   - [ ] $200
   - [ ] $100
   - [ ] $293
   - [ ] none of the above

7. Whenever Steve wants to ask a question about his account, he should mention his account number.

   What is Steve's account number?
   - [ ] 4372 4171
   - [ ] A-473-241
   - [ ] can't tell from the statement

Here is part of what is written on the back of Steve's statement:

In Case of Errors or Inquiries About Your Bill

Send your inquiry in writing on a separate sheet so that the creditor receives it within 60 days after the bill was mailed to you. Your written inquiry must include:
1. Your name and account number (if any);
2. A description of the error and why (to the extent you can explain) you believe it is an error; and
3. The dollar amount of the suspected error.

You remain obligated to pay the parts of your bill not in dispute, but you do not have to pay any amount in dispute during the time the creditor is resolving the dispute. During that same time, the creditor may not take any action to collect disputed amounts or report disputed amounts as delinquent.

8. Steve believes he should have been charged $50 for the electronic game he bought, not $100. What does the statement tell him to do?
   - [ ] phone the charge card company
   - [ ] phone the place where he bought the game
   - [ ] write the charge card company
   - [ ] write the place where he bought the game

24. Getting Paid

The law requires companies to take taxes out of their employees' earnings before paying them. So an employee earning $200 a week takes home <u>less</u> than $200 a week.

A pay statement comes with the paycheck and says what was taken out.

NOTICE the kinds of information on the pay statement below.

TOTAL AMOUNT EARNED   AMOUNTS TAKEN OUT   AMOUNT PAY CHEC

PERIOD ENDING	REG.	O.T.	REGULAR	O.T.	COMM.	TOTAL	F.I.C.A.	FEDERAL W. TAX	STATE TAX	CITY TAX	DISAB.	MAJ MED. & DENTAL	BLUE CROSS	NET AMOUNT
3/9/85	25		150.00		—	150.00	9.20	19.60	4.30	---	.60	2.00	2.00	113.30
	HOURS WORKED		EARNINGS		★					DEDUCTIONS				

CODES

NY - NEW YORK
NJ - NEW JERSEY
C - CALIFORNIA
LE - LOANS & EXCHANGES
VAC - VACATION
S - SICK
H - HOLIDAY

MINDY'S TRAVEL AGENCY
4310 CANAL STREET
HERKIMER, N.Y.

EMPLOYEE'S PAY STATEMENT — PLEASE DETACH AND KEEP FOR YOUR TAX RECORD

WORDS AND MEANINGS

O.T.—overtime, hours or earnings more than the regular

comm.—commission, money earned by some salespeople based on how much they sell

deductions—money taken out of earnings

F.I.C.A.—Social Security, a national insurance program that sends a check every month to retired people and certain others who cannot work

Federal W. Tax—Federal Withholding Tax, amount taken out for federal income tax

disab—disability, a program to pay sick or injured workers while they cannot work

Maj. Med. & Dental, Blue Cross— insurance programs to help pay doctor, dentist and hospital bills

QUESTIONS

1. The pay statement on the last page is for 1 week's pay earned by Sally Reyes. Who does it go to?
   ☐ Sally ☐ Sally's employer

2. What were Sally's total earnings before anything was taken out?

   _____

3. How much did Sally take home that week?

   _____

4. How many hours did she work?

   _____

5. Did she earn any overtime?
   ☐ yes ☐ no

6. How much did she earn in commission on sales?
   ☐ $0 ☐ $20 ☐ $130

7. $9.20 was taken out of Sally's earnings for:
   ☐ Income Tax
   ☐ Medical Insurance
   ☐ Social Security

8. How much was taken out of her pay for Federal Income Tax?

   _____

9. In Sally's state, do workers have to pay a State Income Tax?
   ☐ yes ☐ no

10. In Sally's city, do workers have to pay a City Income Tax?
    ☐ yes ☐ no

11. Sally had a car accident. Which deductions go toward insurance plans that will help pay her doctor and hospital bills?
    (Check more than one)
    ☐ Maj. Med. & Dental
    ☐ Blue Cross
    ☐ F.I.C.A.

12. Sally won't be able to go back to work for some time. Which deduction goes toward paying a small income to workers like Sally who cannot work for a while?
    ☐ Disab.
    ☐ Federal W. Tax

SALLY AT WORK

SALLY UNABLE TO WORK

25. Paying Taxes Part 1

Every year you must report your earnings to the Internal Revenue Service, the IRS. This is the U.S. Government's tax office. This report is called an **Income Tax Return.** One is shown on the next page. Separate instructions explain how to fill it out. Forms can be picked up from banks or IRS offices. You can pay a service to make out your tax return. Or you can do it yourself. This lesson will introduce you to the **Federal Income Tax Return.**

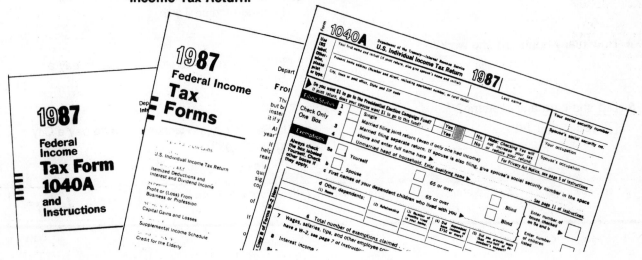

WORDS AND MEANINGS

dependent—a child or other person supported by the taxpayer (There are some special rules about dependents)

interest—money paid you by a bank if you have a savings account

exemptions—allowances that lower the taxes you have to pay

dividends—payments for owning stock in a company

balance due—money you owe

QUESTIONS
(Use the Tax Return on the next page to answer all these questions)

1. Find Line 6 on the Return. Look at the box. What is the **TOTAL NUMBER OF EXEMPTIONS** Ram is claiming?
   ☐ 1   ☐ 2   ☐ 3

2. If everything else is the same, who will pay less tax?
   ☐ person with one exemption
   ☐ person with several exemptions

3. Find Line 5c. How many children live with Ram and depend on him for support?
   ☐ 0   ☐ 1   ☐ 2

4. Line 7 has Ram's salary for the year. Look at Line 8 and 9. Ram earned more than his salary because he
   ☐ had a savings account
   ☐ owned stock in a company
   ☐ worked overtime

5. Read the sentence next to the big arrow. Which did Ram do?
   ☐ let the IRS figure his tax
   ☐ figured his own tax

6. Look at Lines 14 and 15. Which is true?
   ☐ Ram owes the IRS taxes
   ☐ the IRS owes Ram a refund

Form **1040A**

Department of the Treasury—Internal Revenue Service
U.S. Individual Income Tax Return **1987**

Use IRS label. Otherwise, please print or type.

Your first name and initial (if joint return, also give spouse's name and initial)
RAM M. & DENISE T.
Last name **BAHADUR**

Your social security number **518 04 1492**

Present home address (Number and street, including apartment number, or rural route)
513 University Drive

Spouse's social security no. **545 10 1776**

City, town or post office, State and ZIP code
Flagstaff, Arizona 86001

Your occupation **Clerk**

Do you want $1 to go to the Presidential Election Campaign Fund? — Yes ✓ / No
If joint return, does your spouse want $1 to go to this fund? — Yes ✓ / No

Note: Checking Yes will not increase your tax or reduce your refund.

Spouse's occupation **Student**

Filing Status

Check Only One Box

1 ☐ Single
2 ✓ Married filing joint return (even if only one had income)
3 ☐ Married filing separate return. If spouse is also filing, give spouse's social security number in the space above and enter full name here ▶ _____
4 ☐ Unmarried head of household. Enter qualifying name ▶ _____ See page 11 of Instructions.

For Privacy Act Notice, see page 5 of Instructions

Exemptions

Always check the box labeled Yourself. Check other boxes if they apply.

5a ✓ Yourself ☐ 65 or over ☐ Blind
b ✓ Spouse ☐ 65 or over ☐ Blind
c First names of your dependent children who lived with you ▶ **Sushil**

Enter number of boxes checked on 5a and b ▶ **2**

Enter number of children listed ▶ **1**

d Other dependents:

(1) Name	(2) Relationship	(3) Number of months lived in your home.	(4) Did dependent have income of $750 or more?	(5) Did you provide more than one-half of dependent's support?

Enter number of other dependents ▶

6 Total number of exemptions claimed . . . .   Add numbers entered in boxes above ▶ **3**

7	Wages, salaries, tips, and other employee compensation. (Attach Forms W–2. If you do not have a W–2, see page 7 of Instructions)	7	6,200 00
8	Interest income (see page 4 of Instructions)	8	180 00
9a	Dividends _____ 9b Exclusion _____ Subtract line 9b from 9a ▶ (See pages 4 and 8 of Instructions)	9c	
10	Adjusted gross income (add lines 7, 8, and 9c). If under $8,000, see page 2 of Instructions on "Earned Income Credit." If eligible, enter child's name ▶ **Sushil**	10	6,380 00

11a Credit for contributions to candidates for public office. Enter one-half of amount paid but do not enter more than $25 ($50 if joint return). (See page 8 of Instructions) . . . | 11a |

IF YOU WANT IRS TO FIGURE YOUR TAX, PLEASE STOP HERE AND SIGN BELOW.

b Total Federal income tax withheld (if line 7 is larger than $17,700, see page 8 of Instructions) . . . . | 11b | 49 00

c Earned income credit (from page 2 of Instructions) . . . . . | 11c | 162 00

12	Total (add lines 11a, b, and c)	12	211 00
13	Tax on the amount on line 10. (See Instructions for line 13 on page 9, then find your tax in the Tax Tables on pages 14–25.)	13	25 00
14	If line 12 is larger than line 13, enter amount to be **REFUNDED TO YOU** . . . . ▶	14	186 00
15	If line 13 is larger than line 12, enter **BALANCE DUE.** Attach check or money order for full amount payable to "Internal Revenue Service." Write social security number on check or money order . . ▶	15	

Please Attach Copy B of Forms W–2 Here

Please Attach Check or Money Order Here

Please Sign Here

Under penalties of perjury, I declare that I have examined this return, including accompanying schedules and statements, and to the best of my knowledge and belief, it is true, correct, and complete. Declaration of preparer (other than taxpayer) is based on all information of which preparer has any knowledge.

▶ *Ram M Bahadur* 2/18/88
Your signature / Date

▶ *Denise T. Bahadur* 2/18/88
Spouse's signature (if filing jointly, BOTH must sign even if only one had income)

Paid Preparer's Information	Preparer's signature ▶		Preparer's social security no.	Check if self-employed ▶ ☐
	Firm's name (or yours, if self-employed), address and ZIP code ▶		E.I. No. ▶	
			Date ▶	

23-0916750

☆U.S. Government Printing Office:

Form **1040A**

26. Paying Taxes Part 2

Every January your employer should send you a form **W-2** like the one below. It will state your earnings for the past year and list the taxes that were taken out. There will be several copies, one to send with your Federal Tax Return, one to send with your State Return (if your state requires one), and one to keep for your records.

1 Control number		2 Employer's State number			
	22222				For Official Use Only
3 Employer's name, address, and ZIP code		4 Sub-total / Cor-rection / Void			MAKE NO ENTRY HERE
Skokie Steel & Wire 8825 Newberry N.W. Grand Rapids, MI 49504					
		7 Employer's Identification number			
		17-130-2006			
10 Employee's social security number	11 Federal income tax withheld	12 Wages, tips, other compensation	13 FICA tax withheld		14 Total FICA wages
788-22-9942	$967.20	$7,800.00	$478.40		$7,800.00
15 Employee's name (first, middle, last)		16 Pension plan coverage? Yes/No	17 *		18 FICA tips
Roberta L. Laker		NO			
19 Employee's address and ZIP code		20 State income tax withheld	21 State wages, tips, etc.		22 Name of State
1014 Dorrel N.E. Grand Rapids, MI 49505		223.60	7,800.00		MICHIGAN
		23 Local income tax withheld	24 Local wages, tips, etc.		25 Name of locality
		$99.80	$7,800.00		Grand Rapids
Wage and Tax Statement 1987		Copy B to be filed with employee's FEDERAL tax return			
Form W-2		Department of the Treasury—Internal Revenue Service			

WORDS AND MEANINGS

compensation—pay for your work

withheld—taxes or payments taken out of earnings <u>before</u> paying employee

QUESTIONS

1. Copy B of Form W-2 is shown above. What should Roberta do with it?

   ☐ keep it with her records
   ☐ send it to the IRS with her Federal Tax Return

2. Find Number 12 on the W-2. How much did Roberta earn from Skokie Steel & Wire?

   ☐ $967.20   ☐ $7800.00

3. How much Federal Income Tax was taken out?

_____

4. How much was taken out for Social Security?

_____

---

5. At the right is a paragraph from the Instructions for Preparing Form 1040A, the easiest of the Tax Return Forms. It tells how to fill out Line 7 on the Form.

Read the instructions. Take the information from Roberta's W-2 on the last page and FILL OUT line 7 below.

Line 7
Wages, Salaries, Tips, and Other Employee Compensation

Enter the total of all the wages shown on your Forms W–2. Report all wages you received even if you don't have a Form W–2. If all your tips are not shown on your Forms W–2, add these amounts in, too. For a joint return, combine the totals for you and your spouse.

If you lose a Form W–2, ask your employer for a new one. If your employer does not give you a Form W–2 by January 31, or if the one you have is not correct, you should contact your employer as soon as possible. Only your employer can issue your Form W–2 or correct it. If you can't get a Form W–2 from your employer by February 15, contact an Internal Revenue Service office.

FROM INSTRUCTIONS FOR PREPARING FORM 1040A

Forms W				
7	Wages, salaries, tips, and other employee compensation. (Attach Forms W–2. If you do not have a W–2, see page 7 of Instructions)	**7**		

FROM FORM 1040A INCOME TAX RETURN

---

6. Read the instructions for Line 7. Julius Torm has a W-2 for $7,000 from one company. He got another W-2 for $3,000 from another company he worked for. How much would he enter in Line 7?

☐ $3,000   ☐ $7,000   ☐ $10,000

7. Beth is a waitress. She got a W-2 from her restaurant for $6,000. She earned $3,000 in tips, which she has no W-2 for. What should she report on Line 7?

☐ $3,000   ☐ $6,000   ☐ $9,000

8. Anton lost his W-2. What should he do?

☐ ask his company for another copy
☐ fill out Line 7 but not send in the W-2

9. Tim Harriman got a W-2 for $5,000 for his main job. He earned $400 doing part time work and did not get a W-2 for it. How much should he report on Line 7?

☐ $5,000   ☐ $5,400

69

Unit 4 Review

1. Which of the following is a **utility**?

   ☐ electricity
   ☐ furniture
   ☐ clothing

2. Junie Flatt got charged 50¢ on his phone bill for **directory assistance**. What was this charge for?

   ☐ the cost of a long distance call
   ☐ the cost of getting help from a telephone operator in finding a telephone number
   ☐ the cost of calls made to nearby areas

3. Dani Maxwell's latest phone bill had a line that reads, "Balance from last Bill (please disregard this amount if paid) . . . . $10.00."
   What does this mean?

   ☐ Dani is owed $10 by the phone company
   ☐ Dani owes a total of $10 to the phone company on her latest bill
   ☐ Dani owed $10 on last month's bill, but she doesn't have to pay it this month if she has already paid it

4. On June 12, 1985 John Finn writes a check for $20.00 to the Union Gas Company. The check is for his gas bill. His gas **account number** is 73-106-7218.

   Write out the check:

First National Bank	NUMBER _____467_____
	_____19_____
PAY TO THE ORDER OF _____	$ _____
_____ DOLLARS	
	_____
FOR _____	
⑈0 2 ⒑0 ⑊000 ⑈	

5. LuAnne McKim wrote her **endorsement** on a money order. What does this mean?

- ☐ She bought it. She is signing her name on the front
- ☐ She received it. She is signing her name on the back
- ☐ She's asking for a refund. She made it out wrong

6. Where can you buy a **Money Order**?

- ☐ County Clerk's Office
- ☐ Loan Office
- ☐ Post Office

7. A **service charge** is

- ☐ "rent" the bank pays you for using your money
- ☐ money the bank charges you for handling your account

8. On a bank statement, a **closing balance** is

- ☐ the last check you deposited
- ☐ the last deposit you made
- ☐ the amount you had in the bank when the statement was made up

9. The bank **credited** your account with $10. This means that

- ☐ $10 went into your account
- ☐ $10 was taken out of your account
- ☐ $10 was the total amount in your account

Here is a section of Rosa Conti's pay statement:

PERIOD ENDING	REG.	O.T.	REGULAR	O.T.	COMM.	TOTAL	F.I.C.A.	FEDERAL W. TAX	STATE TAX	U.I.	DISAB.	MAJ. MED. & DENTAL	BLUE CROSS	NET AMOUNT
6/17/85	35		215.00			215.00	13.18	24.50	4.30	1.08	1.08	4.00	2.00	164.86
	HOURS WORKED		E A R N I N G S		★					D E D U C T I O N S				

CODES

N Y - NEW YORK
N J - NEW JERSEY
C - CALIFORNIA
L E - LOANS & EXCHANGES
V A C - VACATION
S - SICK
H - HOLIDAY

TOMASEK BAKERIES
2216 State Street
Perth Amboy NJ 08861

EMPLOYEE'S PAY STATEMENT — PLEASE DETACH AND KEEP FOR YOUR TAX RECORD

10. How much money is actually on Rosa's paycheck? $ _____

11. How much federal withholding tax was taken out of her pay? $ _____

12. What is her basic weekly salary, before deductions? $ _____

13. How much social security tax was taken out of her pay? $ _____

14. How much state income tax was taken out of her pay? $ _____

15. Nina and Ted Kolinsky have three children. Two live with them and one has grown up and moved out of the house. On a tax form, how many **dependent** children would they list?

☐ 1 ☐ 2 ☐ 3

16. Sid Weissman claims 4 **exemptions** on his tax form. What does this mean?

☐ he pays more taxes than if he claimed no exemptions

☐ he pays less taxes than if he claimed no exemptions

☐ it doesn't affect the amount of taxes he pays

17. Susan McClean's employer **withheld** $3000. What does this mean?

☐ she was paid $3000

☐ $3000 was taken out of her pay

☐ she owes $3000

18. Eric Hedlund has a Super-Charge card. His statement last month listed a $5.00 **finance charge.** This amount was also part of

☐ the new balance

☐ the purchases

☐ the previous balance

19. When Eric's monthly Super-Charge statement was made out, the **total amount** he owed was listed as

☐ previous balance

☐ purchases

☐ payments

☐ finance charge

☐ new balance

☐ minimum payment due

Unit V.
AGREEMENTS AND GUARANTEES

When you sign an agreement, it means two things. It means you agree to what the agreement says. And it means you understand what it says. Even if you don't really understand it, or didn't even read it properly, you have agreed to it. You must do what it says.

There are lots of times you sign an agreement. When you buy something on credit. When you rent a place to live. In fact, just about every time someone gives you a piece of paper with writing on it for you to sign, you are being asked to sign an agreement.

Knowing how to read an agreement lets you know what you are getting into. It's an important part of Life Skills Reading.

CONTENTS OF THIS UNIT

27. Guarantees

READ the Warranty Card below. (A warranty is
the same as a guarantee.)

NOTICE the kinds of information on both the front and back.

LOOK UP words you don't know in the WORDS AND MEANINGS.

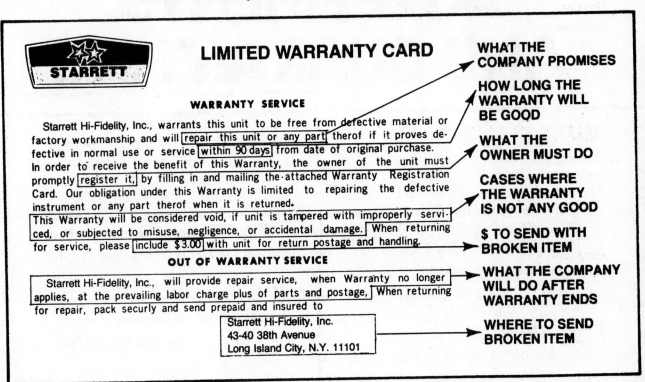

LIMITED WARRANTY CARD

STARRETT

WHAT THE
COMPANY PROMISES

HOW LONG THE
WARRANTY WILL
BE GOOD

WHAT THE
OWNER MUST DO

CASES WHERE
THE WARRANTY
IS NOT ANY GOOD

$ TO SEND WITH
BROKEN ITEM

WHAT THE COMPANY
WILL DO AFTER
WARRANTY ENDS

WHERE TO SEND
BROKEN ITEM

WARRANTY SERVICE

Starrett Hi-Fidelity, Inc., warrants this unit to be free from defective material or factory workmanship and will repair this unit or any part therof if it proves defective in normal use or service within 90 days from date of original purchase. In order to receive the benefit of this Warranty, the owner of the unit must promptly register it, by filling in and mailing the attached Warranty Registration Card. Our obligation under this Warranty is limited to repairing the defective instrument or any part therof when it is returned. This Warranty will be considered void, if unit is tampered with improperly serviced, or subjected to misuse, negligence, or accidental damage. When returning for service, please include $3.00 with unit for return postage and handling.

OUT OF WARRANTY SERVICE

Starrett Hi-Fidelity, Inc., will provide repair service, when Warranty no longer applies, at the prevailing labor charge plus of parts and postage, When returning for repair, pack securly and send prepaid and insured to

Starrett Hi-Fidelity, Inc.
43-40 38th Avenue
Long Island City, N.Y. 11101

Important Information to owners

Before returning instrument for repair, please be sure to pack properly and securely and insure with your carrier against loss or breakage.

Please be sure to mail warranty card immediately for registration of warranty.

Your sales slip must accompany unit. Speakers do not have to be returned unless defective.

IMPORTANT: Please DO NOT send batteries with unit for service as possible corrosion can result in expensive damage not covered by Warranty. Accessories such as microphones, Earphones, etc. should only be returned if there is reason to believe accessory item is cause of trouble. A letter should be included stating the exact problem you are having. This will enable us to serve you more efficiently.

For purchases made in the United States, mail card to
Starrett Hi-Fidelity, Inc.
43-40 38th Avenue
Long Island City, N.Y. 11101

MORE FOR
THE OWNER
TO DO

WORDS AND MEANINGS

void—not any good

tampered with or improperly serviced—you or someone who was not approved by the company tried to fix the item

insure—buy insurance

misuse—using it wrong

negligence—being careless

abuse—harming it

warranty or **guarantee**—a promise to fix or replace something you buy if it doesn't work

QUESTIONS

1. Jan Kramer of 147 Oak St., Tampa, Florida, bought a Starrett tape recorder on May 1, 1985. He got it at Sound Heaven, 2130 Snelling Ave., Tampa, Florida. The tape recorder came with the warranty shown on the previous page and a warranty registration card (right).

   Fill in the warranty registration card for Jan.

2. What should Jan do with the card?
   ☐ keep it in a safe place
   ☐ mail it

LIMITED WARRANTY REGISTRATION CARD

Model #CR205 Date of Purchase _____

Owner's name _____

Owner's address _____

Dealer's name _____

Dealer's address _____

City-State _____

Please Print
Please fill out this card and mail immediately

Look at the Warranty Card on the last page to answer Questions 3-6

3. Can Jan get the tape recorder fixed for free?
   On July 8?   ☐ yes   ☐ no
   On Sept. 5?   ☐ yes   ☐ no

4. Which will get repaired for free?
   ☐ a friend worked on it when it wouldn't start
   ☐ Jan knocked it off a table.
   ☐ it stopped while recording some music from the radio

5. What must Jan do when he sends the tape recorder back for repairs? (Check more than one)
   ☐ buy insurance for it
   ☐ pack it well
   ☐ put in $3.00
   ☐ put in sales slip
   ☐ put in registration card
   ☐ take out batteries

6. Which is better—a guarantee or a warranty?
   ☐ guarantee
   ☐ warranty
   ☐ no difference

28. Credit Agreements

Lots of buying is done on credit. In credit buying, you buy an item and agree to pay for it later. Usually, you'll pay something each month until you have paid off what you owe. Here are some common kinds of buying on credit:

charge account at a store

an **installment plan** purchase of a sofa

time payments for an auto

charge card or **credit card** purchases

a "**Buy now—Pay later**" vacation

When you buy on credit, you'll have to sign a legal paper called a Credit Agreement. A sample Credit Agreement is shown below.

READ the sample agreement carefully. If you don't know what some of the words mean, look them up in the WORDS AND MEANINGS.

CREDIT AGREEMENT

Your signature below means that you agree to the following terms:

1. When you get a monthly statement you must pay at least the **MINIMUM AMOUNT DUE** by the **NEXT BILLING DATE.**

2. A **FINANCE CHARGE** will be added to your bill every month. This will be a percentage of your balance. It includes interest and all service charges.

3. The Monthly Rate for the **FINANCE CHARGE** is 1.5%. The Annual or Yearly Rate is 18%.

4. You can pay the entire balance before the **NEXT BILLING DATE.** If you do you will pay no **FINANCE CHARGE.** You also can pay any amount between the **MINIMUM AMOUNT DUE** and the entire balance.

5. If you fail to pay at least the **MINIMUM AMOUNT DUE,** we have the right to declare all obligations due.

Applicant's Signature   Date

Co-Applicant's Signature   Date

WORDS AND MEANINGS

statement—a monthly bill that shows what you have already paid and how much you still owe

minimum amount due—you must pay at least this amount. You may pay more if you want to

billing date—date on which the store sends you a bill or statement

finance charge—an extra amount added to your bill in addition to the costs of whatever you charged. It often consists of interest plus service charges (see below)

previous balance—what you owed last month

interest—extra money you agree to pay back when you borrow or buy on credit. It's like rent for using the borrowed money

service charges—fees to cover the expenses of handling your account, sending out bills, etc.

new balance—what you owe this month

pay your obligations—pay the minimum amount due shown on the statement

declare all obligations due—demand payment of all the money you owe

QUESTIONS

1. Read Paragraph 1 of the Credit Agreement.

   The billing date on Barry Feldman's charge card statement is always the 15th of the month. He got a statement saying, "Billing Date, April 15. Minimum Payment Due, $20.00." Which of the following is OK to do?

   ☐ pay $15 before May 1, and no more
   ☐ pay $20 on May 5
   ☐ wait till May 29 and pay $30

2. Read Paragraphs 2 and 3 of the Agreement.

   Velma Franklin's previous balance is $100. The finance charge for the month will be

   ☐ 1.5% of $100
   ☐ 18% of $100
   ☐ no finance charge

3. Read Paragraph 4 of the Agreement.

   Patsy Kubecka has a new balance of $60. Her minimum payment is $5.00. How can she avoid paying a finance charge on the new balance?

   ☐ pay $60 before the next billing date
   ☐ pay $5.00 before the next billing date

4. Read Paragraph 5 of the Agreement.

   Pete O'Hara fails to make his monthly payment of $10 on a $200 debt. The store has a right to

   ☐ collect $10 only
   ☐ collect the full $200 right away

5. Travis Charles's father, Owen Charles, is a co-applicant on Travis's credit agreement. Travis can't make his payments. The company may collect from

   ☐ Travis only
   ☐ Owen

6. Who will pay more in finance charges?

   ☐ Edgar Rodriguez, who owed $100 and paid it back in 2 months
   ☐ Karen Jorgensen, who owed $100 and paid it back in 10 months

7. Look at this part of a Note (a special kind of Credit Agreement) that Gregg Alder signed when he borrowed $500 from his bank.

   Besides repaying the $500, now much extra does he have to pay for using the money?

   $ _____

First National Bank

Borrower		Date of Note
GREGG ALDER		12/5/85
47 BEACON PLACE		
BLACKDUCK MN 56630		

Amount of Loan	First Installment Due	Final Installment Due
$500.00	1/2/86	1/2/87
Interest	**Total to be Repaid**	**Number of Monthly Installments**
$60.00	$560.00	12

29. Reading A Lease Part 1

When you rent an apartment you will probably have to sign a lease. The lease is a paper which says what you and the landlord agree to. Usually leases are very long and hard to read. But if you understand what's in them you can protect yourself better.

Below is the top part of a lease.

NOTICE what Paul Marten is agreeing to pay and for how long.

T 186— Apartment lease, 2-5 familly dwelling, plain English format, 12-78

PREPARED BY ARNOLD MANDELL, L.L.B.

© 1978 BY JULIUS BLUMBERG, INC., PUBLISHER, NYC 10013

LEASE AGREEMENT

The Landlord and Tenant agree to lease the Apartment at the Rent and for the Term stated on these terms:

LANDLORD: Jaybee Leasing Inc.
Address for Notices: 750 Ocean St
Portland, Maine

TENANT: Paul Marten
5240 State Street
Gorham, Maine

Apartment (and terrace, if any) 4B at 153 High Street, Portland, Maine

Lease date: March 19 85	Term 1 Year beginning April 1 19 85 ending March 31 19 86	Yearly Rent $ 2400 Monthly Rent $ 200 Security $ 200

Rider Additional terms on..............page(s) initialed at the end by the parties is attached and made a part of this Lease.

1. Use
The Apartment must be used only as a private Apartment to live in and for no other reason. Only a party signing this Lease and the spouse and children of that party may use the Apartment.

2. Failure to give possession
Landlord shall not be liable for failure to give Tenant possession of the Apartment on the beginning date of the Term. Rent shall be payable as of the beginning of the Term unless Landlord is unable to give possession. Rent shall then be payable as of the date possession is available. Landlord will notify Tenant as to the date possession is available. The ending date ... will not change.

WORDS AND MEANINGS

tenant—person who lives in a rented place

landlord—person who owns the place that a tenant rents

term—period of time when the lease is in effect

eviction—when a landlord gets a court order that lets him put the tenant <u>out</u> of an apartment

security—extra money that the tenant pays to the landlord before moving in. The money is for any damage the tenant may do or for any rent the tenant may fail to pay. If nothing is wrong, the tenant should get the security back when he or she moves

pay in advance—pay for something before you use it

QUESTIONS Look at the lease above to answer these questions.

1. How long is Paul's lease for?

☐ 1 year ☐ 2 years

2. On what date does the lease end?

_____

3. How much has Paul agreed to pay every month?

_____

4. How much has Paul agreed to pay in total? Since the lease is for 1 year, copy this amount from the **Yearly Rent.**

_____

5. Rent is supposed to be paid <u>in advance</u>. When must Paul pay April's rent?

☐ by April 1   ☐ by May 1

6. When Paul signed the lease, he agreed to rent for 1 year and pay $2400. If Paul leaves after paying 6 months rent, the landlord can go to court to make him pay $1200.

If you want to move after a few months, you should look for an apartment

☐ with a lease   ☐ with no lease

7. A tenant can get evicted for not doing what the lease says. Can Paul be forced to give up his apartment if he doesn't pay $200 every month?

☐ yes   ☐ no

8. How much security did Paul give the landlord before he moved in? $_____

9. Paul's kids marked up the walls in the apartment. He couldn't get the markings off. So when Paul moved out, the landlord held back part of the money Paul had put up as

☐ rent   ☐ security

What the landlord found when Paul moved out

10. The lease also protects the tenant. If the tenant does what the lease says, the landlord must usually wait until the lease ends to ask him or her to move or to raise the rent.

If a tenant thinks a landlord is doing something illegal, he or she should get a lawyer or a city agency to help.

Nona Berger has a lease and has done what it says. Her landlord is trying to evict her. What should she do?

☐ call a lawyer
☐ pay no attention to anything the landlord tries

**Know what you are signing
Pay your rent on time
Get help when you need it**

30. Reading A Lease Part 2

Laws about leases are different in every city and state. Even in the same city, leases will be different. When you read a lease, look for what could cause you trouble.

Below are a few paragraphs from Mason Taylor's lease.

NOTICE that they all say what the tenant <u>cannot</u> do.

NOTICE also that one paragraph has been crossed out.

1. USE
This apartment may only be used as space for living and for no other purpose. Only the person signing this lease and his or her immediate family may live in the apartment.

2. PETS
~~Tenant must not keep pets in the apartment.~~   *J. Cobb*   M.T.

3. ASSIGNMENT AND SUBLEASE
Tenant may not sublet any part of the apartment or permit anyone else to use it without Landlord's written permission. If tenant does, it is a default, and Landlord has the right to cancel the lease.

4. ALTERATIONS
Tenant must get written permission from Landlord to paint or wallpaper the apartment, or to make any alterations. Tenant must not make any changes in the plumbing, electric, or heating systems.

WORDS AND MEANINGS

party—a person

spouse—husband or wife

alteration—changing an apartment in a way that makes it hard or expensive to change back

sublease or **sublet**—when a tenant rents an apartment to someone else

prior written consent—getting a written "OK" before doing something

cancel the lease—end the tenant's right to the apartment; evict him

default—failure to live up to an agreement

QUESTIONS

1. Read Paragraph 1 of Mason Taylor's lease. What does it say about his running a TV repair shop in the apartment?

☐ he can   ☐ he can't

2. Look back at paragraph 1. Who can live in the apartment? (Check more than 1 answer)

☐ Mason   ☐ Mason's friends
☐ Mason's wife   ☐ Mason's children

3. Look at Paragraph 2. It used to say "No Pets." Mason asked Mr. Cobb, the landlord, to take it out. Mr. Cobb agreed. How was this change made? (Check more than one)

☐ old paragraph crossed out
☐ change initialed or signed by tenant
☐ change initialed or signed by landlord
☐ entire lease rewritten

4. Read Paragraph 3. Mason asked the landlord to take it out and add one saying he could sublet. The landlord said "No." Mason signed the lease anyway. Which is a <u>default</u>?

☐ Mason keeps a dog in the apartment
☐ Mason rents the apartment to a friend for a while

5. What does "cancel the lease" mean in Paragraph 3?

☐ evict or try to evict the tenant
☐ raise the rent

6. Before a landlord evicts a tenant he usually sends a warning. This gives a tenant a few days to correct the problem. Mason was late with the rent. He got a warning and quickly paid it all. Will he be evicted?

☐ yes   ☐ no

7. Read Paragraph 4. Mason thinks the walls are ugly. The landlord says he won't paint them. Which picture shows an alteration that requires Mason to get a written OK from the landlord before he starts?

☐ Picture 1   ☐ Picture 2

PUTTING UP
A PICTURE

PICTURE 1

PICTURE 2

PUTTING UP
WALLPAPER

Unit 5 Review

Questions 1-6 are based on the Warranty Card shown below.

1. Matt Hyland bought a Maxivox radio. The radio came with the Warranty Card shown below. Matt asks you if the Warranty Card is as good as a guarantee. What do you tell him?

   ☐ a Warranty Card is better
   ☐ a guarantee would be better
   ☐ they're the same

2. Matt bought the radio on Jan. 2. The radio stopped playing on March 7. Is the warranty still good?

   ☐ yes   ☐ no

3. Matt is thinking of trying to fix the radio himself. Which is true?

   ☐ the warranty states that Matt must try to fix it before sending it in
   ☐ Matt may try to fix it if he wishes
   ☐ Matt must not try to fix it, or the warranty is no good

4. Matt sends the defective radio to Maxivox along with a description of what's wrong. What else must he send?

   ☐ complaint slip from the store where he bought it
   ☐ sales slip from the store where he bought it
   ☐ warranty card

5. The trouble with Matt's radio was a defective transformer. It took 20 minutes to replace. What will Maxivox charge Matt?

   ☐ the cost of the transformer
   ☐ the labor cost for replacing the transformer
   ☐ nothing

6. Suppose the radio had stopped because Matt's little brother had dropped it. Would the warranty take care of fixing it?

   ☐ yes   ☐ no

90-DAY LIMITED WARRANTY

This Maxivox equipment is warranted to be free from defects in material or workmanship for 90 days from date of delivery. Repair (or at our our option, replacement) will therefore be made of any unit which proves to be defective during this period, provided the unit is returned properly packed, with all transportation charges prepaid, to the Maxivox factory in Rhode Island. Any repair approved hereunder will be made without charge to the owner for parts or labor. This warranty extends only to the original purchaser and is not transferable.

Claims under this warranty must be accompanied by the original sales slip to establish date of purchase.

This warranty does not extend to units which have been subjected to misuse, abuse, neglect, accident or to units that have been used in violation of operating instructions.

Equipment which, in our judgement, shows evidence of having been altered, modified, or serviced without our authorization, or which has had its serial number altered or removed, will be ineligible for service under warranty.

MAXIVOX RADIO ELECTRONICS
121 Route 46 Metawasket R.I.

7. **Interest** on borrowed money means
   - ☐ the money you borrow
   - ☐ "rent" you pay on borrowed money
   - ☐ the amount you repay each month

8. A **finance charge** is most like
   - ☐ a balance
   - ☐ interest
   - ☐ a statement

9. Verna Di Stefano gets a letter from a store where she has a charge account. The letter states that if she doesn't pay her monthly bill soon, the store "will declare all obligations due." What does this mean?
   - ☐ she'll have to return what she bought
   - ☐ she'll owe the whole amount of her bills right away, and won't be allowed to pay in installments
   - ☐ she'll be put in jail

10. On a charge account statement, the total amount you owe is called
    - ☐ service charge
    - ☐ new balance
    - ☐ previous balance

11. Whose finance charge was larger?
    - ☐ Andy Schwenk, who owed $500 and took 2 years to pay it back
    - ☐ Mildred Zukoff, who owed $500 to the same store and took 4 months to pay it back.

12. Brock Morganfield applies for a loan. His brother Todd is a co-applicant. What would happen if Brock got the loan and couldn't pay it back?
    - ☐ Brock would go to jail
    - ☐ Todd would have to pay
    - ☐ the bank would lose its money

13. Les Turner rents an apartment from Sheila Cobb. Who is the **tenant**?
    - ☐ Les
    - ☐ Sheila

14. Yolanda Carson is renting an apartment for $200 a month. The landlord, Mr. Waters, wants a month's security. What is he asking for?
    - ☐ money to pay for locks on the doors and windows
    - ☐ money that he'll keep only if she damages the apartment or doesn't pay the rent

15. Nina Moran gets an **eviction** notice. This means
    - ☐ she has a written lease
    - ☐ the landlord is trying to make her leave
    - ☐ she is getting an increase in her rent

CHECK NUMBER _102_   **First National Bank**   50-264 / 213

DATE ___May 1___ 19_87_

PAY TO THE ORDER OF _Horace Waters_ $_200 00/_

Two Hundred and No/00 _____ DOLLARS

For _Security_   _Yolanda Carson_

⑆0 2 13=0 264⑈

The remaining questions refer to the sections of the lease shown below.

16. How long is the lease for?
    ☐ 1 year
    ☐ 2 years

17. What is the monthly rent for the apartment?
    ☐ $3000
    ☐ $200
    ☐ $250

18. When is the June rent due?
    ☐ on the first day of June
    ☐ any day in June
    ☐ on the last day of June

19. Sylvia Grasso signed this lease on the Lease date written in on the form. When is the May rent due? (Read Section 3 carefully)
    ☐ April 15
    ☐ May 1
    ☐ May 15
    ☐ May 31

20. After one year exactly, Sylvia Grasso misses one month's payment. Look at the end of Section 3 of the lease. What does the lease say the landlord has the right to do?
    ☐ collect $250 only
    ☐ collect $500 the next month
    ☐ demand $3000

T 186— Apartment lease, 2-5 familly dwelling, plain English format, 12-78

PREPARED BY ARNOLD MANDELL, L.L.B.

© 1978 BY JULIUS BLUMBERG, INC., PUBLISHER, NYC 10013

LEASE AGREEMENT

The Landlord and Tenant agree to lease the Apartment at the Rent and for the Term stated on these terms:

LANDLORD: **Herbert Kuo**   TENANT: **Sylvia Grasso**

Address for Notices: **37 East Shore Drive**   **12 N. Randle Street**
Klamath Pass, OR   **McMurfree, OR**

Apartment (and terrace, if any) at **14 Pastor Place, Klamath Pass**

Lease date: **Apr 15** 19 **84**	Term **2 years** beginning **May 1** 19 **84** ending **April 30** 19 **86**	Yearly Rent $ **3000** Monthly Rent $ **250** Security $ **250**

Rider   Additional terms on .... page(s) initialed at the end by the parties is attached and made a part of this Lease.

1. Use
    The Apartment must be used only as a private Apartment to live in and for no other reason. Only a party signing this Lease and the spouse and children of that party may use the Apartment.

3. Rent, added rent
    The rent payment for each month must be paid on the first day of that month at Landlord's address. Landlord need not give notice to pay the rent. Rent must be paid in full and no amount subtracted from it. The first month's rent is to be paid when Tenant signs this Lease. Tenant may be required to pay other charges to Landlord under the terms of this Lease. They are to be called "added rent." This added rent is payable as rent, together with the next monthly rent due. If Tenant fails to pay the added rent on time, Landlord shall have the same rights against Tenant as if Tenant failed to pay rent. Payment of rent in installments is for Tenant's convenience only. If Tenant defaults, Landlord may give notice to Tenant that Tenant may no longer pay rent in installments. The entire rent for the remaining part of the Term will then be due and payable.

ployees.
29. Paragraph headings   The Paragraph headings are for convenience only.
30. Changes   This Lease may be changed only by an agreement in writing signed by and delivered to each party.
31. Effective date   This Lease is effective when Landlord delivers to Tenant a copy signed by all parties.

Unit VI.
FILLING OUT FORMS AND APPLICATIONS

Whenever you apply for a driver's license, or a social security number, or even a job, you'll have to fill out a form.

If you want to get a credit card, or open a bank account, or buy something from a mail-order catalog, you'll have to fill out a form.

Unfortunately, may people aren't careful enough when they read the forms they fill out. They fill the forms out wrong. And so, they end up having to apply more than once to get a driver's license. They don't get that job they were trying for. The credit card company won't give them credit. And they get the wrong merchandise from the catalog house.

Knowing how to read and fill out forms and applications is a vital life skill in today's world.

CONTENTS OF THIS UNIT

31. Ordering By Mail

Below is a part of a page from a mail order catalog.

NOTICE the pictures of the 2 styles and the facts you need for filling out the order form.

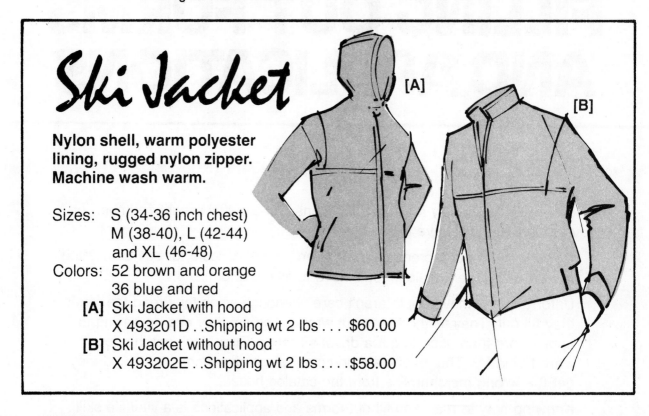

Ski Jacket

Nylon shell, warm polyester lining, rugged nylon zipper. Machine wash warm.

Sizes: S (34-36 inch chest)
   M (38-40), L (42-44)
   and XL (46-48)
Colors: 52 brown and orange
   36 blue and red
 [A] Ski Jacket with hood
  X 493201D ..Shipping wt 2 lbs $60.00
 [B] Ski Jacket without hood
  X 493202E ..Shipping wt 2 lbs $58.00

WORDS AND MEANINGS

account number—number a company gives to a person to use in all business the person does with the company

C.O.D.—**C**ollect **O**n **D**elivery (or **C**ash **O**n **D**elivery); the person who delivers an item collects payment for it.

QUESTIONS

1. Read Section 1 of the order form on the opposite page. This section should be filled out by a customer who has
   ☐ a complaint   ☐ a charge account

2. Notice how Section 2 is filled out. At the time of her last order, Stella's name and address were Stella Ford, 16-10 Taney Lane, Kankakee, IL. 61625. Fill out Section 4 of the order form for her.

3. Section 3 should be filled out only if the order is going to
   ☐ the address in Section 2
   ☐ a different address

4. Look at Section 5. Stella has already ordered 3 jackets. She wants to order another. On the next blank line, write her order for a ski jacket <u>without</u> a hood, for a man with a <u>42-inch chest</u>. Make it <u>blue and red</u>.

5. This is not a **CREDIT ORDER.** Which section should be filled out?

☐ 6   ☐ 8

6. Add the **MAILING WEIGHTS.** $(4+2+2+=?$ pounds) Fill in this number for the **TOTAL WEIGHT** in Section 8.

7. Add the **TOTAL PRICES.** $(\$116+\$60+\$58=?)$ Fill in this number in the space for **MERCHANDISE TOTAL** in Section 8.

8. A table called a rate schedule on p.221 of the catalog says mailing 8 pounds to Peoria costs $2.44. Fill in this amount in the space for **MAILING.**

9. Illinois' 5% **SALES TAX** on this order equals $11.70. Fill this in.

10. Add up all the $ in Section 8. Fill this number in the space for **TOTAL $ ENCLOSED.**

11. Read Section 7. How should Stella pay for the jackets?

☐ pay the person who delivers them
☐ send a check

T.C.Fox ORDER FORM

TODAY'S DATE:

1 YOUR T.C. FOX CHARGE ACCOUNT NUMBER, IF ANY (MUST BELONG TO NAME AT RIGHT).

PLEASE PRINT

2 NAME STELLA CARTER
NO./STREET 2810 LAZY LN.   APT. NO. 2D
CITY/STATE PEORIA, IL   ZIP 61611
AREA CODE 309   HOME PHONE NO. 752-4844

3 SEND TO: (IF DIFFERENT FROM NAME & ADDRESS IN SECTION 2.)

NAME
NO./STREET   APT. NO.
CITY/STATE   ZIP

4 FILL OUT THIS SECTION IF ABOVE NAME & ADDRESS HAVE CHANGED SINCE LAST ORDER.

FORMER NAME
PREVIOUS NO./STREET   APT. NO.
CITY/STATE   ZIP

5 NAME OF ITEM	HOW MANY	CATALOG NUMBER	SIZE	COLOR & COLOR NO.	PRICE FOR ONE		TOTAL PRICE		MAILING WEIGHT
SKI JACKET	2	X493202E	M	blue/rd 36	59	00	116	00	4 lbs
SKI JACKET	1	X493201D	S	brown/or 52	60	00	60	00	2 lbs

6 CREDIT ORDER (CHARGE ACCOUNT)	**7** CASH ORDER (NON-CHARGE ACCOUNT)	**8** FILL OUT AMOUNTS IF SENDING PAYMENT		TOTAL WEIGHT
		MERCHANDISE TOTAL		⬇
☐ THIS IS A REGULAR CHARGE PURCHASE	PAY BY CHECK OR MONEY ORDER ONLY. DO NOT SEND STAMPS OR CURRENCY.	MAILING SEE RATES P. 221		
☐ THIS IS A TIME PAYMENT PURCHASE		SALES TAX		
SIGNATURE	NO C.O.D. ORDERS	TOTAL $ ENCLOSED		

32. Addressing Envelopes

NOTICE the kinds of information on the envelope below.

Also NOTICE where the information is written.

RETURN ADDRESS

Mark Arcardi
3200 Tulip Drive
Accident, Md 21520

15¢

Ms. L. B. Sanchez ——————— NAME
Service Department ——————— PART OF COMPAN
Baker Hi-Fi ——————— NAME OF COMPA
421 Cliff Cave Rd. ——————— NUMBER & STREE
St. Louis, Mo. 63129 ——————— CITY & STATE
ZIP CODE

WORDS AND MEANINGS

Zip Code—number that helps the Post Office find an address

return address—address of person who sends the letter

QUESTIONS

1. Rick Lester is visiting his aunt. His letters are sent to her mail box, in care of her name, Mrs. Ellen Bell. Look at Rick's address, right. What is the abbreviation for <u>in care of</u>? _____

2. Draw a circle around the apartment number in Rick's address.

Rick Lester
c/o Mrs. Ellen Bell
Apt. 2B
210 Tall Oak Dr.
Aurora, IL 60505

RICK'S ADDRESS

3. Betty Largo gets her mail in a box at the Crosstown Station Post Office. Which are in her address?

☐ name of post office and box number
☐ name of street and house number

Betty Largo
P.O. Box 4444
Crosstown Station
Memphis, TN
38104

BETTY LARGO'S ADDRESS

4. The L&R Bag Company is at 21 Gold Road in Acton, California.

The list at the right is from the Zip Code Directory. That's a book found in every Post Office. Circle the zip code for Acton on the list.

CALIFORNIA
(Abbreviation: CA)
Acampo . .95220
Acton 93510
Adelanto . .92301
Adin 96006

FROM THE ZIP CODE DIRECTORY

5. What abbreviation for California is given in the Zip Code Directory?

☐ CA   ☐ CAL   ☐ CALIF

6. Address the envelope below to Steve Lacy. He is in the Shipping Department of the company in Question 4. Use your own address for the return address.

33. Applying For A Social Security Number

Just about everybody who has a job, or pays income taxes, or gets social security checks from the government, has a social security number. You'll need to get one too someday if you don't already have one.

You can apply for a social security number at your local Social Security Office by filling out a form like this one:

LOOK carefully at the front of the form. (The back has special directions on how to fill it out.)

ID: CN: DO: 183

APPLICATION FOR A SOCIAL SECURITY NUMBER
See Instructions on Back.   Print in Black or Dark Blue Ink or Use Typewriter.

DO NOT WRITE IN THE ABOVE SPACE

1. Print FULL NAME YOU WILL USE IN WORK OR BUSINESS   (First Name)   (Middle Name or Initial—if none, draw line _____)   (Last Name)

2. Print FULL NAME GIVEN YOU AT BIRTH

6. YOUR DATE OF BIRTH   (Month) (Day) (Year)

3. PLACE OF BIRTH   (City)   (County if known)   (State)

7. YOUR PRESENT AGE (Age on last birthday)

4. MOTHER'S FULL NAME AT HER BIRTH (Her maiden name)

8. YOUR SEX   MALE   FEMALE

5. FATHER'S FULL NAME (Regardless of whether living or dead)

9. YOUR COLOR OR RACE   WHITE   NEGRO   OTHER

10. HAVE YOU EVER BEFORE APPLIED FOR OR HAD A UNITED STATES SOCIAL SECURITY, RAILROAD, OR TAX ACCOUNT NUMBER?   NO   DON'T KNOW   YES   (If "Yes" Print **State** in which you applied and **Date** you applied and **Social Security Number** if known)

11. YOUR MAILING ADDRESS   (Number and Street, Apt. No., P.O. Box, or Rural Route)   (City)   (State)   (Zip Code)

12. TODAY'S DATE

NOTICE: Whoever, with intent to falsify his or someone else's true identity, willfully furnishes or causes to be furnished false information in applying for a social security number, is subject to a fine of not more than $1,000 or imprisonment for up to 1 year, or both.

13. TELEPHONE NUMBER   14. Sign YOUR NAME HERE (Do Not Print)

DHEW, Social Security Administration
Form **SS-5** (5-78)

☐ RESCREEN ☐ ASSIGN ☐ DUP ISSUED   Return completed application to nearest SOCIAL SECURITY ADMINISTRATION OFFICE

Form Approved OMB No 72-R0571 No social security number may be issued unless this form is completed (26 CFR. Part 31.6011(b)-2)

WORDS AND MEANINGS

with intent to falsify—planning to lie, not just making a mistake

willfully—on purpose

furnishes false information—lies

QUESTIONS

1. Look at the directions above Line 1 of the form.

   Which of the following can you use to fill out the form? (Check more than one)

   ☐ pen with light blue ink
   ☐ pen with black ink
   ☐ pencil
   ☐ typewriter

2. Look at the directions on Line 1 of the form.

   Which of the following is the correct way to fill out Line 1?

   ☐ KAREN SCHWARTZ
   ☐ SCHWARTZ, KAREN
   ☐ Karen Schwartz
   ☐ Karen ——— Schwartz

3. Look at the directions on Lines 1 and 2.

Walter McCarthy's real name is Leo Walter McCarthy, but he never uses the "Leo." What name should he put on Line 2?

☐ Leo Walter McCarthy
☐ L.W. McCarthy
☐ Walter McCarthy

4. Look at the directions on Line 4.

Tessa Frame's mother was born Sue-Ellen Last. When she married, she became Sue-Ellen Frame. What name should Tessa write on Line 4?

☐ Sue-Ellen Frame
☐ Sue-Ellen Frame Last
☐ Sue-Ellen Last

---

5. Look at the directions above Line 1 and on Line 5. Then look at this direction on the back of the form:

5 If a stepfather, adopting father, or foster father is shown, include the relationship after name; for example, "John H. Jones, stepfather."

Norm Oliveira lives with his mother and his stepfather, who has adopted him. He isn't sure how to list his stepfather. What should he do first?

☐ don't list the stepfather at all
☐ write "stepfather" after the stepfather's name
☐ ask the Social Security Office for instructions
☐ write the stepfather's name and nothing more

---

6. Peggy Laxalt once applied for a social security number when she lived in Montana. She can't find the card or the number, and she doesn't know the exact date. Which way should she fill out her form?

☐ A   **10** HAVE YOU EVER BEFORE APPLIED FOR OR HAD A UNITED STATES SOCIAL SECURITY, RAILROAD, OR TAX ACCOUNT NUMBER?   NO ☐   DON'T KNOW ☐   YES ☒ → (If "Yes" Print **State** in which you applied and **Date** you applied and **Social Security Number** if known)   Montana | unknown | unknown

☐ B   **10** HAVE YOU EVER BEFORE APPLIED FOR OR HAD A UNITED STATES SOCIAL SECURITY, RAILROAD, OR TAX ACCOUNT NUMBER?   NO ☐   DON'T KNOW ☒   YES ☐ → (If "Yes" Print **State** in which you applied and **Date** you applied and **Social Security Number** if known) | |

---

7. Look at the directions for Line 14.

Which is the correct way for Roosevelt Styles to fill in Line 14?

☐ ROOSEVELT STYLES
☐ Styles, Roosevelt
☐ Roosevelt Styles

---

8. Amalia Morel is applying for a social security card for her 2-year-old son, Gabriel. (She is putting some money in a bank account for him, and the bank needs his social security number.)

Read the instructions for Line 14, which are printed on the back of the application form.

How should the form be signed?

☐ Gabriel Morel
☐ X
☐ Amalia Morel, mother

14 Sign your name as usually written. Do not print unless this is your usual signature. (If unable to write, make a mark witnessed by two persons who can write. The witnesses preferably should be persons who work with the applicant and both must sign this application.) A parent, guardian, or custodian who completes this form on behalf of another person should sign his own name followed by his title or relationship to the applicant, for example, "John Smith, father."

9. Fill out the social security application form on the last page. Use facts about yourself. Or if you wish, make up facts about someone else.

34. Applying For A Driver's License

Below is a Driver's License Application form for the State of Virginia. **NOTICE** that there are spaces for name, address, birth date, and social security number.

Many forms ask for this same information. But they don't always want it written the same way. On the form below, do they want you to write your last name first or last? Do they want you to write your address on one line or on three?

DIVISION OF MOTOR VEHICLES-RICHMOND, VA.

APPLICATION FOR

- [ ] OPERATOR'S
- [ ] CHAUFFEUR'S
- [✓] INSTRUCTION
- [ ] RENEWAL
- [ ] ORIGINAL
- [ ] REISSUE
- [ ] DUPLICATE

FEE $ **3.00** 0 228

FILL IN INFORMATION ON FRONT AND BACK WITH INK OR TYPEWRITER

If you wish to be licensed to operate one or more of the vehicles described below check block(s) indicating desired class, and answer question(s).

- [ ] CLASS A – Truck or tractor truck over 40,000 lbs.
- [ ] CLASS B – Passenger bus-more than 32 seats.
   Have you driven this class vehicle at least 500 miles? Yes ____ No ____
- [ ] CLASS C – Motorcycle
- [ ] CLASS S – School bus   } Prior driving experience does not exempt any qualifying test.

REASON FOR DUPLICATE
- [ ] LOST
- [ ] STOLEN
- [ ] DESTROYED

If your name has changed since last license was issued, show below name on your present license.

NAME:

PRINT FULL NAME	FIRST	MIDDLE	LAST	
PRINT STREET ADDRESS OR RFD NO.				
PRINT CITY OR POST OFFICE				
		STATE	ZIP CODE	
PRINT CITY OR COUNTY OF RESIDENCE	SEX	WEIGHT	HEIGHT	EYE COLOR
			FT. IN.	
HAIR COLOR	DATE OF BIRTH		YOUR SOCIAL SECURITY NO.	
	MONTH DAY YEAR			

ALL RENEWAL APPLICANTS READ CAREFULLY

PLEASE APPEAR AT THE EXAMINING STATION TO COMPLETE ANY EXAMINATION(S) REQUIRED BY LAW. IF YOU ARE UNABLE TO COMPLY, OR IF THE EXAMINING STATION IN YOUR AREA IS NOT SCHEDULED TO BE OPEN ON THE DATE OF APPOINTMENT (SEE ENCLOSED SCHEDULE), YOU MAY APPEAR AT ANY TIME DURING YOUR BIRTH MONTH IN THE YEAR OF RENEWAL.

DMV USE ONLY

	PASS	FAIL
VISION	[ ]	[ ]
WRITTEN	[ ]	[ ]
ROAD	[ ]	[ ]

APPLICANT QUALIFIES FOR CLASS A [ ] B [ ]
C [ ] S [ ]

APPOINTMENT DATE

EXAMINATION

FS REQUIREMENT

PART A [ ]
PART B [ ]
PHOTO [ ]
NO PHOTO [ ]

STATION NO. _____ DATE _____

DMV USE ONLY

FSR (W) _____ FSR (R) _____

Form DLIA Rev. 4/77

WORDS AND MEANINGS

instruction license (sometimes called a **learner's permit**)—license to drive for a person who knows the rules but needs to practice before taking a driver's test on the road. Only good when a licensed driver is in the car

operator's license—regular driver's license

chauffeur's license—a license to drive others as part of a job for pay. A taxi driver would need this kind of license

convicted of an offense—found guilty by a court, not just arrested or given a ticket

duplicate license—copy of a lost or stolen license

visual condition—something wrong with eyesight

impairs—harms

suspended—taken away for a time

revoked—taken away

fee—an amount of money that must be paid

QUESTIONS

1. Look at the top of the form on the last page. Notice which box is checked. What kind of license is wanted?

   ☐ copy of a lost license
   ☐ learner's license to practice driving
   ☐ regular license to drive

   How much must you pay to get this license?

   _____

2. Look over the rest of the left side of the form. Notice that none of the items is for new drivers who want to learn to drive a car.

   Now look at the right side. Find the spaces for name, address, hair color, date of birth, social security number, etc. Fill all these spaces in on the form, using facts about yourself.

   If you do not have a middle name, draw a line like this (⤙⤙⤙⤙) between your first and last names. Then it will be easy to see you did not just skip over this part of the form.

   If you do not have a social security number, just for this lesson use 431-22-6895.

3. The back of the application is shown below. Notice Item 1 at the left. The most common reason to check "yes," is "need glasses." Notice that if you answer "yes," you need to explain your answer on the line provided.

   Now answer Item 1 below.

4. Answer Items 2 and 3. Most new drivers will answer "no." If you have to answer "yes," be sure to explain it under Item 3.

5. Answer Item 4. If you have no other license, draw lines through the spaces.

6. Answer Item 5.

7. Write your social security number in the box. If you have none, use 431-22-6895 just for this lesson. Be careful to keep the dashes (-) in the right places.

8. Sign your name in the box and fill in the name of your city or county and today's date at the bottom of the form. Follow directions carefully!

9. Notice the blanks on the right for the signature of parent or guardian. When does a parent or guardian have to sign?

   ☐ every application
   ☐ when applicant is under 18
   ☐ when applicant is under 21

ANSWER ITEMS 1 THRU 5 AND FURNISH OTHER INFORMATION REQUESTED | Answer Yes or No

1. Do you have a visual, physical or mental condition that impairs your ability to drive? _____
   If so, explain _____

2. Have you been convicted within the past ten years in this state or elsewhere of any _____
   offense resulting from your operation of or involving a motor vehicle?

3. Has your license or privilege to drive been suspended or revoked in this state or elsewhere? _____
   If the answer to question 2 or 3 is "yes" show court, date and kind of offense(s). List each separately _____

4. Show in space provided below any valid out of state license held by you.
   State _____ License No. _____

5. FOR INSTRUCTION PERMITS ONLY: Do you know that this license only permits _____
   operation while you are accompanied by a licensed driver?

SOCIAL SECURITY OR CONTROL NO.

NO PART OF YOUR SIGNATURE OR SOCIAL SECURITY NUMBER SHOULD APPEAR OUTSIDE OF THE BOXED LINES ON THIS CARD.

__ __

APPLICANTS WRITTEN SIGNATURE __ __ __ __

I HEREBY CERTIFY THAT ALL INFORMATION IN THIS APPLICATION IS TRUE AND CORRECT.

EXECUTED AND SIGNED IN THE CITY/COUNTY OF _____ MO___ DAY___ YEAR___

APPLICANTS UNDER 18 YEARS OF AGE

I hereby give consent for issuance of drivers license to the named applicant who is at least sixteen years of age (15 years 8 months for instruction permits) and under eighteen years.

PARENT _____

GUARDIAN _____

1. Have you ever been found not innocent of any offense in a juvenile and domestic relations | Yes or No
   court in this or any other state? _____

2. IF ANSWER TO QUESTION 1 IS "YES" THE INFORMATION BELOW MUST BE COMPLETED BY THE COURT.

   IT IS MY OPINION THAT THE SUBJECT'S REQUEST FOR A LICENSE TO OPERATE MOTOR VEHICLES SHOULD _____ SHOULD NOT _____ BE GRANTED.

   REMARKS

COURT

SIGNATURE _____ TITLE _____

FOR OFFICE USE ONLY

IBM E46440

93

35. Applying For A Job

There are many different kinds of job application forms. But whenever you fill one out, you must read it carefully to find out exactly what it wants. If you don't read the directions and fill out the form properly, it could cost you a job.

Below is a section of an application form. Look it over.

NOTICE what things are asked for.
NOTICE what things the form asks you to list first and what it asks you to list last.

APPLICATION FOR EMPLOYMENT

COMPLETE IN INK; PLEASE PRINT

LAST NAME (1)	FIRST	MIDDLE	SOCIAL SECURITY NO.	DATE PREPARED

ADDRESS – NO.	STREET	CITY	STATE	ZIP	HOW LONG AT PRESENT ADDRESS?

MARITAL STATUS (SINGLE, MARRIED, WIDOWED, DIVORCED OR SEPARATED) (2) — NO. OF CHILDREN (3) — NO. OF OTHER DEPENDENTS (4) — PHONE NO. — YEARS MOS.

DRIVERS LICENSE NO. — STATE — DATE EXPIRES — TRAFFIC VIOLATIONS (WITHIN LAST 3 YEARS) (5)

EDUCATION AND TRAINING

SCHOOL	NAME AND LOCATION	FROM MO./YEAR	TO MO./YEAR	YEAR COMPLETED	DID YOU GRADUATE?
Grammar				7 8	
High				1 2 3 4	
College or University				1 2 3 4	

WORK EXPERIENCE (List previous employers, starting with most recent, whether part or full-time)

EMPLOYER	ADDRESS No. STREET / City STATE	FROM MO./YR.	TO MO./YR.	JOB DESCRIPTION / SUPERVISOR'S NAME	SALARY RATE	REASON FOR LEAVING
1 (6)				(7) (8)		
2						
3						

SPECIAL SKILLS

(9)

REFERENCES (Give names of at least 2 PERSONS (local, if possible) who have known you over 3 years. Omit relatives.)

NAME	ADDRESS	BUSINESS	HOW LONG KNOWN YOU?
(10)			

WORDS AND MEANINGS

dependents—people you support by paying their living expenses or taking care of them

traffic violation—driving in a way that's against the law, and getting a traffic ticket for it. Parking violations are not traffic violations

employer—a company or person you work for. It's not the same as a supervisor or boss, who directs your work and who also works for the employer

supervisor—your boss, the person who tells you what to do on the job

reference—the name of someone who can recommend you for a job and say good things about you

local—living nearby

omit—leave out

special skills—things you can do that a job might be able to use, like operating special machinery or speaking more than one language

---

QUESTIONS

1. Look at the Blank Number 1. Which is the correct way for John Jerome Gilligan to fill it in?

   ☐ *John Jerome Gilligan*

   ☐ GILLIGAN, JOHN JEROME

   ☐ John Jerome Gilligan

2. Freda Stuben supports her mother. What is the number of the blank where she should put this information?

   ☐ 2   ☐ 4
   ☐ 3   ☐ no blank

3. One year ago, Bill Hartz got a ticket for parking in a loading zone. Does he have to put this down in Blank Number 5?

   ☐ yes   ☐ no

4. Susan Tohei goes to Molton High School. Before that, she went to Glenmore Grammar School. Which should she list first?

   ☐ Molton   ☐ Glenmore

5. Look at the heading **WORK EXPERIENCE.** Read what comes after it. Susan worked at Dorsey Mail Enterprises last summer. Right now she has a part-time job at the Paukis Tissue Paper Company. Which should she list first?

   ☐ Dorsey Mail
   ☐ Paukis Tissue

6. Susan works as a part-time quality control inspector for Paukis. Where should she put this information?

   ☐ in Blank No. 6
   ☐ in Blank No. 7
   ☐ in Blank No. 8
   ☐ on a separate sheet of paper

7. Susan was hired at Paukis Tissue Paper by Ms. Elaine Terrell, who was also her boss. Where should Susan list Ms. Terrell's name?

   ☐ in Blank No. 6
   ☐ in Blank No. 8

8. A family friend, Mr. Kay Fusaki, is willing to recommend Susan for a job. Where should Susan list him?

   ☐ in Blank No. 8
   ☐ in Blank No. 10
   ☐ on a separate sheet of paper

9. Look at the heading **REFERENCES.** Read what comes after it.

   Which of the following would also be a good reference for Susan to list? (Check only one.)

   ☐ Mr. Kagan, neighbor for the last year and a half
   ☐ Mrs. Fuller, school librarian, has known Susan for 4 years
   ☐ Mr. Shimada, Susan's uncle, has known Susan all her life

36. Applying For Credit

Michie Chenier wants a charge card. Then she can shop when she wants and pay the bills the next month. If the credit card company thinks she can and will pay her bills, they will send her the card.

LOOK over the first two parts of the application form, below, that Michie filled out.

PART 1. YOU AND YOUR WORK

Applicant's Last Name: CHENIER, First Name: MICHELLE Initial: L.	Birth Date: MAY 5, 1955	Social Security Number: 223-59-7878
Home Phone: 394-4447	No. Dep. Children: 2	Driver's License No: 432-71-48 State: GEORGIA
Street Address: 2104 La Vista Ave.	How Long: 1 YEAR	Applicant's Employer: M&G APPLIANCE Mthly. Income: $1300
City: Atlanta State: GEORGIA	Zip Code: 30324	Employer's Address: 71 JOHNSON FERRY RD., Atlanta
Previous Address: 2029 Whitlock Ave. S.W., Marietta, Georgia	How Long: 3 YRS	Business Phone: 471-4821 Position: APPLIANCE REPAIR How Long Yrs. 2 Mos.
Name of Nearest Relative not living with you/Relationship: MRS. TRACEY LEWIS / MOTHER		Previous Employer: How Long
Address of Relative Named Above: 1410 STRAWBERRY LANE, DECATUR, GEORGIA		Previous Employer's Address: Date Left

Other Income (Describe): SELF-EMPLOYED APPLIANCE REPAIR

NOTE: If Alimony, Child Support or Separate Maintenance, you are not required to include this income if you do not plan to rely on it to pay this account. See Part 3. Other Income Amount $200/mo

If you are paying alimony, child support or separate maintenance, how much of your income is so obligated? $ NONE

Total Monthly Income $ 1500

PART 2. YOUR FINANCIAL REFERENCES

Bank with: UNION STATE BANK, 5220 EAST MOUNTAIN St., Atlanta
☒ Checking Acct. No. 432-781-4328
☒ Savings Acct. No. 72436-3781
☐ Loan Acct. No.
☐ Charge Card No.

Savings and Loan: Office/Address:
☐ Savings
☐ Loan — List Below

Credit Union: Office/Address:
☐ Savings
☐ Loan — List Below

MONTHLY EXPENSES: LIST BELOW ALL OBLIGATIONS NOW OWING INCLUDING CHARGE CARDS — Attach Separate List if Necessary.

	Name & Address to whom Payments are/were made. (If NONE, list paid accounts)	Account Number	Original Amount	Balance Owed	Monthly Payment
☐ Buying ☒ Renting ☐ Live w/Parents	ELLIOT TEPPER, MERRIMAC CO., 320 JOHNSTON FERRY RD.		$	$	$ 350
AUTO: Year 1983 Make FORD	VALLEY FORD, 3100 EMORY RD. NE ATLANTA, GEORGIA	321-42-871			
OTHER					

WORDS AND MEANINGS

obligations—money owed

alimony—money paid after divorce by husband or wife to support the other

separate maintenance—same as alimony, except the couple are separated but not divorced

child support—money paid after divorce or separation to support children

contractually responsible—signed an agreement; must pay bills or be forced to pay by a court

PART 3.

COMPLETE THIS PART ONLY WHEN:	A. Husband/Wife/other Co-Applicant is contractually responsible for the account or B. You are relying on Alimony, Child Support or Separate Maintenance as "Other Income"		

HUSBAND/WIFE OR FORMER HUSBAND/WIFE OR OTHER CO-APPLICANT VERNON CHENIER	RELATIONSHIP TO APPLICANT (IF ANY) HUSBAND	SOCIAL SECURITY NO. 432-75-4241

EMPLOYER ACE SEMICONDUCTORS, INC.	OCCUPATION MAINTENANCE TECHNICIAN	HOW LONG 3 YEARS	NET MONTHLY INCOME $ 1200

EMPLOYER'S ADDRESS 2240 PLASTER RD.	CITY ATLANTA	STATE GEORGIA	BUSINESS PHONE 821-4842

Name and Address of Husband/Wife/other Co-Applicants Relatives

READY RESERVE: I request that READY RESERVE deposits be made to my C&S or Participating Bank checking account in multiples of $50, up to my line of credit. ☐ **Yes** ☑ **No**

I affirm the foregoing answers are true and complete. I authorize you to obtain such information as you may require concerning the statements made in this application. I understand that the C&S Charge Card(s) for which I am making application, is/are governed by and subject to the Customer Agreement set forth on the reverse hereof, which I have read. I understand I will be sent a full disclosure of the terms governing the use of this account and a disclosure of my rights to dispute billing errors upon final approval of the account.

Please issue ☐ one ☐ two C&S Charge Cards, and C&S Master Charge® Cards.

DATE	SIGNATURES x _Michelle L. Chenier_ APPLICANT x _Vernon R. Chenier_ CO-APPLICANT	SIGNATURE OF OTHER AUTHORIZED USERS: x _Anita Chenier_ x _____	RELATIONSHIP mother-in-law

QUESTIONS

1. Fill in the following information about Michie's last job: Michie used to work at Keen's Home Heating at 47 Tucker Rd., Atlanta. She worked there for 3 years and left Oct. 5, 1982.

2. Michie makes about $200 a month extra money repairing appliances outside her regular job. She fills in this amount in the part of the form called
   - ☐ Other Income
   - ☐ Previous Employer

3. Now look at PART 2 of the form. Which two things did Michie need to know before she could fill out PART 2?
   - ☐ name of person who gets her rent
   - ☐ checking account number
   - ☐ name of president of her bank

4. Michie is buying a car from Valley Ford. Fill in the following information on the form:
   The car cost $6000
   Michie still owes $1000
   She pays $100 every month

5. A Co-Applicant is the same as an applicant. Both can use the charge card. Both are equally responsible for paying the bills. Who is the Co-Applicant in PART 3 above?
   - ☐ Michie's mother-in-law
   - ☐ Michie's husband

6. What does it mean to say that Vernon is "contracturally responsible"?
   - ☐ He is a responsible person and usually pays his bills
   - ☐ He signed a promise to pay, and if he does not, the company can go to court to get the money

7. Whose income and employer does the form ask about?
   - ☐ only Michie's
   - ☐ both Michie's and her husband's

8. An Authorized User can use the card to buy things, but does not have to pay the bills. Who can use the card and not pay the bill?
   - ☐ Michie's husband
   - ☐ Michie's mother-in-law

9. Susan Birch is applying for a credit card. Her husband sends her $600 for separate maintenance every month. She lists that under Other Income in PART 1. Where does she have to list his employer and income?
   - ☐ PART 1
   - ☐ PART 2
   - ☐ PART 3
   - ☐ nowhere

Unit 6 Review

1. Mark Keyser is writing to Shenstone, Inc. It's a mail order house in Laconia, NH. Shenstone gets its mail at P.O. Box 7382. The Zip Code of Laconia is 03246.

   Mark lives in Baytown, TX. His home is on 13 Decker Drive. The Zip Code is 77520.

   Address the envelope. Write in the return address as well as the address to which the envelope is going.

2. You want to order the following products from the Shenstone mail-order catalog:

   Three Canvas Tote Bags, Number S-3278, for $10.00 each
   A Sheath Knife, Number S-7296, for $20.00
   One Pocket-Size Binoculars, Number B-1098, for $50.00

   Write up the order on the order form. Use your own name, street address, and phone number but write "Dennis, MA 02638" for the city / state / zip. (Be sure to follow what the form says about Massachusetts sales tax.)

   You are not shipping by air.

SHENSTONE
P.O. Box 7382, Laconia, NH 03246

ORDERED BY: If there is no PEEL OFF ADDRESS LABEL on the back cover please print your name and address below   DATE_____

☐ MR
☐ MRS _____
☐ MISS ,
☐ MS

STREET ADDRESS _____ APT NO_____

CITY_____

PHONE NUMBER _____ _____

If you have moved since your last order, please give your old address below:

STREET _____ CITY _____ STAT_____ ZIP_____

PRODUCT NUMBER	HOW MANY	NAME OF ITEM	PRICE EACH Dollars / Cents	TOTAL PRICE Dollars / Cents

PACKING AND GUARANTEED DELIVERY:
Orders to be shipped to the U.S.A. its territories or possessions to **EACH** shipping address please add

Orders up to $10.00	$1.55
Orders from $10.01 to $15.00	$2.15
Orders from $15.01 to $25.00	$2.70
Orders from $25.01 to $50.00	$3.55
Orders from $50.01 to $100.00	$4.95
Orders over $100.00	$5.95

MERCHANDISE TOTAL

ADD FOR PACKING AND GUARANTEED DELIVERY

FOR AIR SHIPPING ADD **$2.95** EXTRA

BECAUSE OF OUR STORE LOCATIONS. WE ARE REQUIRED BY LAW TO COLLECT SALES TAX ON THE MERCHANDISE TOTAL FOR SHIPMENTS TO MASSACHUSETTS – 5%, NEW JERSEY – 5%, PENNSYLVANIA – 6%

TOTAL AMOUNT (PLEASE — NO CASH, STAMPS OR C.O.D.'S)

3. Fill out the following application for a credit card.

If you do not have a social security number, use 138-46-9703 as your number.

If you do not have a job, use the following set of facts. You have worked for 2 years 1 month as a hospital attendant at Otistown General Hospital, located at 23 Loring Avenue in your home town. You make $700 a month. The hospital phone number is 928-7600. This is your first job.

If you have no credit references of your own, use the following set of facts. You have a checking account at Otistown National Bank, Number 3-0761. You have a savings account, Number 27-13, at the same bank. You live with your parents, do not owe money on an auto, and have no other credit cards.

CREDICARD APPLICATION

1. Tell us about yourself (ACCOUNT WILL BE SET UP IN NAME OF PERSON COMPLETING THIS SECTION)

LAST NAME	FIRST NAME	INITIAL	BIRTH DATE	TELEPHONE NUMBER	
STREET ADDRESS		APT. NO.	AT PRESENT ADDRESS YRS. MOS.	EDUCATION [ ] HIGH SCHOOL [ ] PART COLLEGE [ ] COLLEGE DEGREE	
CITY	STATE	ZIP CODE	SOCIAL SECURITY NO.		
PREVIOUS ADDRESS		APT. NO.	AT PREVIOUS ADDRESS YRS. MOS.	[ ] RENT [ ] BUYING [ ] LIVE W/PARENTS	
CITY	STATE	ZIP CODE		AGES OF DEPENDENTS	
NAME AND ADDRESS OF NEAREST RELATIVE NOT LIVING WITH YOU				TELEPHONE NUMBER	

2. Tell us about your job

IF RETIRED, ATTACH SHEET LISTING AMOUNT. NAME & ADDRESS OF EACH SOURCE OF INCOME AND ACCOUNT NUMBERS IF APPLICABLE

NAME OF COMPANY	POSITION	YRS. MOS
STREET ADDRESS	BUSINESS TELEPHONE	MONTHLY JOB INCOME
CITY STATE ZIP CODE	PREVIOUS EMPLOYER	
PREVIOUS EMPLOYER ADDRESS	POSITION	YRS. MOS.
SOURCE OF OTHER INCOME (INCOME FROM ALIMONY, CHILD SUPPORT OR SEPARATE MAINTENANCE PAYMENTS NEED NOT BE REVEALED IF YOU DO NOT CHOOSE TO HAVE IT CONSIDERED IN THIS APPLICATION)		MONTHLY AMOUNT

3. Tell us about your credit references

CHECKING ACCOUNTS BANK	SAVINGS ACCOUNTS BANK		LANDLORD	MO. PAYMENTS
ACCT. #	ACCT. #			

LIST BANKS, DEPARTMENT STORES, FINANCE COMPANIES (INCL. ALIMONY AND CHILD SUPPORT OBLIGATIONS) USE ADD'L. SHEET IF NECESSARY

NAME OF CREDITOR	BRANCH OR LOCATION	ACCOUNT NUMBER	BALANCE	MO. PAYMENT
AUTO FINANCED BY				
MORTGAGE HOLDER				

Applicant's Signature	Date

4. Fill out the following job application form. If you have no social security number use 138-46-9703 as your number. For employment history, if you have never held a job, use the same set of facts given in the previous exercise on filling out a credit card application.

PERSONAL (Discrimination because of age, race, creed, color or sex is prohibited by law.)

LAST NAME	FIRST	MIDDLE	MAIDEN

PRESENT ADDRESS	CITY & STATE	TELEPHONE NO.

DATE OF BIRTH	HT.	WT.	SEX		SOCIAL SECURITY NO.

U.S. CITIZEN?	If you are not a U.S. citizen, do you have the legal right to remain permanently in the U.S.?	MARITAL STATUS	AGES OF CHILDREN

OTHER DEPENDENTS?	FATHER'S OCCUPATION	DO YOU OWN A CAR?	DO YOU: ☐ RENT? ☐ BOARD? ☐ OWN HOME?

DATE OF LAST MEDICAL EXAMINATION?	GENERAL HEALTH ☐ POOR ☐ FAIR ☐ GOOD	DAYS OFF WORK (OR LOST FROM SCHOOL) LAST YEAR FOR ILLNESS

PHYSICAL HANDICAPS, IF ANY	HAVE YOU BEEN HOSPITALIZED DURING LAST FIVE YEARS? IF YES, GIVE DETAILS

IN CASE OF EMERGENCY, NOTIFY	RELATIONSHIP

ADDRESS	TELEPHONE NO.

EMPLOYMENT HISTORY

NAME OF EMPLOYER 1)	ADDRESS	DATE STARTED
YOUR POSITION		SALARY

EDUCATION

	NAME AND LOCATION OF SCHOOL	NO. OF YEARS ATTENDED	WHEN DID YOU LEAVE?	GRADUATED: DEGREE	COURSE OR MAJOR	GRADE AVERAGE
HIGH SCHOOL						
COLLEGE						
GRADUATE STUDY						
BUSINESS OR TRADE						

REFERENCES (NOT FORMER EMPLOYERS OR RELATIVES)

NAME	ADDRESS AND PHONE NO.	OCCUPATION
1)		
2)		

Unit VII
SAMPLE FORMS

The next several pages contain a number of different blank forms. Many are similar to those you filled out in earlier units of this book. Others are somewhat different. Still others contain sections that you would not fill out. (You wouldn't fill out the doctor's section of a health insurance form, for example.)

Each form is a real one—an example of a type you may be filling out some time in your own life. Becoming familiar with forms like these is an important part of Life Skills Reading.

CONTENTS OF THIS UNIT

POST OFFICE CHANGE OF ADDRESS FORM

CHANGE OF ADDRESS ORDER

MAIL OR DELIVER TO POST OFFICE OF <u>OLD</u> ADDRESS

AFFIX
FIRST-
CLASS
POSTAGE
IF MAILED

To _____**POSTMASTER**_____

City _____

State _____ ZIP _____

☆ U.S. GPO: 1978—753-331

THIS ORDER PROVIDES for the forwarding of first-class mail and all parcels of obvious value for a period not to exceed 1 year.		Print or Type *(Last Name, First Name, Middle Initial)*	
CHANGE OF ADDRESS IS FOR: ☐ Entire Family *(When last name of family members differ, separate orders for each last name must be filed)* ☐ Individual Signer Only	**OLD ADDRESS**	No. and St., Apt., Suite, P.O. Box or R.D. No. (In care of)	
I AGREE TO PAY FORWARDING POSTAGE FOR MAGAZINES FOR 90 DAYS ☐ NO ☐ YES		Post Office, State and ZIP Code	
USPS USE ONLY CLERK/ CARRIER ENDORSEMENT	**NEW ADDRESS**	No. and St., Apt., Suite, P.O. Box or R.D. No. (In care of)	
		Post Office, State and ZIP Code	
CARRIER ROUTE NUMBER		Effective Date	If Temporary, Expiration Date
DATE ENTERED		Sign Here ▶	Date Signed

PS Form 3575, May 1978 | *Signature & title of person authorizing address change. (DO NOT print or type)*

CHARGE ACCOUNT
APPLICATION

5	2	8	1								
4	3	4	1								

Master Charge/Visa Application

T Trust Company Bank

AP_____ DL_____ CL_____ CD_____

I Prefer a ☐ MASTER CHARGE ☐ VISA ☐ BOTH

I Prefer a Credit Limit of	**Financial**
or Please Increase My Present Limit to	Social Security No.
on Card Number	Driver's License No.
Personal	Bank with
Full Name (First, Middle, Last) Birthdate	☐ Checking ☐ Saving ☐ Loan ☐ Other
Address Apt. No.	Checking Account No. Saving Account No.
City/State Zip	Mortgage or Rent Payable to
Yrs. at Present Address Telephone	Year and Make of Auto(s)
Own or Buying ☐ Rent ☐ Live with Relatives ☐	1. 2.
Previous Address	Financed by
	1. 2.
City/State How Long	**Bank Credit Cards**
No. of Children Ages	Name Acct. No.
Last School Attended	Credit Limit Balance
Education Level Completed Diploma/Degree	Name Acct. No.
Name of Nearest Relative Not Living With You Telephone	Credit Limit Balance
Address	**Other Credit References**
City/State Relation	☐ RICH'S ☐ DAVISON'S ☐ SEARS ☐ PENNEY'S
Employment	Others
Employed by How Long	Company Location
Address	Acct. No. Payment
City/State Zip	Company Location
Position Telephone	Acct. No. Payment
Previous Employer	Company Location
How Long	Acct. No. Payment
Ending Salary	**Monthly Expenses**
Income Alimony, child support, or separate maintenance income need not be revealed if you do not wish to have it considered as basis for repaying this obligation.	Mortgage or Rent Payment $
	Automobile(s) Payment $
Your Monthly Salary or Wages $	Total Other Payments $
Describe Other Income $	Total Monthly Expenses $
Total Monthly Income $	

Please Read Before Signing

This statement is submitted to obtain credit and I certify that all information herein is true and complete. I also authorize the bank to obtain further information concerning my credit standing. The undersigned agrees to the terms and conditions set forth in your cardholder agreement.

Date _____ Number of cards desired ☐ One ☐ Two

Applicant's Signature _____   Joint Obligor's Signature _____

103

APPLICATION TO WORK AT POST OFFICE

INSTRUCTIONS TO APPLICANTS

Furnish all the information requested on these cards. The attached card will be returned to you with sample questions and necessary instructions, including the time and place of the written test.

TYPEWRITE OR PRINT IN INK. DO NOT SEPARATE THESE CARDS. FOLD ONLY AT PERFORATION.

MAIL OR TAKE THIS FORM—BOTH PARTS—TO THE POSTMASTER OF THE POST OFFICE WHERE YOU WISH TO BE EMPLOYED.

☆ U.S. GPO: 1978-785-780/1799 9-1

LAST NAME	FIRST NAME	MIDDLE INITIAL

ADDRESS (House Number and Street)

CITY	STATE	ZIP CODE

BIRTH DATE (Mo., Day, Year)

DATE OF THIS APPLICATION	TELEPHONE NUMBER	DO NOT WRITE IN THIS SPACE

TITLE OF EXAMINATION

WHERE DO YOU WISH TO TAKE WRITTEN TEST (City & State)

PS Form **2479A** May 1978   **APPLICATION CARD**

TITLE OF EXAMINATION	DATE OF THIS APPLICATION	WHERE DO YOU WISH TO TAKE WRITTEN TEST (City & State)
DATE OF BIRTH	SOCIAL SECURITY NUMBER POST OFFICE APPLIED FOR	

IF YOU HAVE PERFORMED ACTIVE DUTY IN THE ARMED FORCES OF THE UNITED STATES AND WERE SEPARATED UNDER HONORABLE CONDITIONS INDICATE PERIODS OF SERVICE FROM
(Mo., Day, Yr.)   TO (Mo., Day, Yr.)

DO YOU CLAIM VETERAN PREFERENCE?   ☐ NO   ☐ YES IF YES, BASED ON

☐ (1) ACTIVE DUTY IN THE ARMED FORCES OF THE U.S. DURING WORLD WAR I OR THE PERIOD DECEMBER 7, 1941, THROUGH JULY 1, 1955, (2) MORE THAN 180 CONSECUTIVE DAYS OF ACTIVE DUTY (OTHER THAN FOR TRAINING) IN THE ARMED FORCES OF THE U.S. AFTER JANUARY 31, 1955, OR (3) AWARD OF A CAMPAIGN BADGE OR SERVICE MEDAL.

☐ YOUR STATUS AS (1) A DISABLED VETERAN OR A VETERAN WHO WAS AWARDED THE PURPLE HEART FOR WOUNDS OR INJURIES RECEIVED IN ACTION, (2) A VETERAN'S WIDOW WHO HAS NOT REMARRIED, (3) THE WIFE OF AN EX-SERVICEMAN WHO HAS A SERVICE-CONNECTED DISABILITY WHICH DISQUALIFIES HIM FOR CIVIL SERVICE APPOINTMENT, OR (4) THE WIDOWED, DIVORCED OR SEPARATED MOTHER OF AN EX-SERVICE SON OR DAUGHTER WHO DIED IN ACTION OR WHO IS TOTALLY AND PERMANENTLY DISABLED

PRINT OR TYPE YOUR NAME AND ADDRESS

FIRST, MIDDLE, MAIDEN, IF ANY, AND LAST NAME

NUMBER AND STREET, OR R.D., OR POST OFFICE BOX NO.

CITY, STATE, AND ZIP CODE (ZIP CODE MUST BE INCLUDED)

DO NOT WRITE IN THIS SPACE

THIS CARD WILL BE RETURNED TO YOU.
BRING IT WITH YOU WHEN YOU REPORT FOR THE WRITTEN TEST.

PS Form **2479B** May 1978   **ADMISSION CARD**

APPLICATION FOR UNEMPLOYMENT BENEFITS

STATE DEPARTMENT OF LABOR - Unemployment Insurance Division

ORIGINAL CLAIM FOR BENEFITS

PLEASE PRINT ALL ENTRIES. PRESENT YOUR SOCIAL SECURITY ACCOUNT CARD WITH THIS FORM

---

1. SOCIAL SECURITY ACCOUNT NUMBER ▶

DO NOT WRITE IN THE BOX BELOW

2. NAME: FIRST   MIDDLE INITIAL   LAST

L.O.

3. ADDRESS: NO.   STREET   APT.

Date

CITY, TOWN, POST OFFICE   COUNTY   ZIP CODE

Eff.
Date

4. AGE

5. Show _how many_ people are dependent on you for at least half of their support. (Do not count yourself)

Spouse_____   Children under 18_____   Other_____   Total (if none enter zero) _____

6a. CIRCLE HIGHEST SCHOOL GRADE COMPLETED:

Grade School   High School   College
0 1 2 3 4 5 6 7 8   9 10 11 12   13 14 15 16 17+

b. Are you attending school now?   ☐ Yes ☐ No

c. Date last attended if within last year   MO. / DAY / YR.

7. What is your present marital status? Check one

☐ Never Married ☐ Married ☐ Divorced ☐ Separated ☐ Widowed

	YES	NO		YES	NO
8. Have you applied for unemployment insurance benefits in this or any other office in the past 52 weeks?	☐	☐	13. Are you receiving, or will you receive vacation or holiday pay during your present period of unemployment?	☐	☐
9. Do you expect to go back to work for your last employer? If "Yes" how soon?_____	☐	☐	14. Do you have any business or are you engaged in any other activity that brings in or may bring in income?	☐	☐
10. Was there a strike, lockout or other labor dispute in any place where you worked during the last 8 weeks?	☐	☐	15. Are you related in any way to any of the persons for whom you worked or performed any services during the past 12 months?	☐	☐
11. Do you belong to a union? If "Yes" enter name and local._____	☐	☐	16. Within the last 12 months have you worked for a corporation of which you were an officer?	☐	☐
12. Have you applied for or are you receiving:			17. Did you work under a different name during the last 12 months?	☐	☐
a. pension or retirement payment?	☐	☐	If "Yes" what name?_____		
b. social security benefits?	☐	☐	18. Are you a citizen of the United States?	☐	☐
c. workmen's compensation or disability benefits?	☐	☐			

19. LIST ALL YOUR EMPLOYERS DURING THE PERIOD **FROM** _____ **THRU** _____

START WITH YOUR LAST EMPLOYER and work back. Failure to list all your employers and Federal service (civilian and military) may result in a reduced benefit rate or a delay in your benefits. **YOUR EMPLOYERS WILL BE NOTIFIED THAT YOU FILED A CLAIM!**

DATES	NAME OF LAST EMPLOYER	_DO NOT WRITE IN ANY OF THE SPACES BELOW._
A BEGAN WORK MO. DAY YR.		
	STREET ADDRESS	
LAST DAY WORKED MO. DAY YR.	CITY STATE ZIP CODE CLOCK NO.	E.R. No.
	OCCUPATION ON THIS JOB WORK LOCATION. IF MARITIME WORKER SHOW ARTICLE NO. & NAME OF SHIP	

	Weeks	Wages	
Total			E'
Under $40			or
Net			C
Other:			

I AM NOT WORKING FOR MY LAST EMPLOYER BECAUSE:

IF YOU WORKED FOR ADDITIONAL EMPLOYERS DURING THE ABOVE PERIOD, PLEASE USE THE OTHER SIDE OF THIS FORM. ➡

I hereby register for work and claim unemployment insurance benefits. I certify that I am now unemployed, that I am ready, willing and able to work and that the statements I have made in this application are true and correct. I understand that the law provides severe penalties for wilful false statements to obtain benefits.

CLAIMANT SIGN HERE ▶ _____

105

JOB APPLICATION

CBS PERSONNEL RECORD

CBS POLICY AND FEDERAL AND STATE LAWS FORBID DISCRIMINATION BECAUSE OF AGE, COLOR, RACE, RELIGION, SEX OR NATIONAL ORIGIN. IF YOU ARE APPLYING FOR A POSITION IN THE FIELD OF BROADCASTING AND BELIEVE YOU HAVE BEEN DISCRIMINATED AGAINST FOR THE ABOVE, YOU MAY NOTIFY THE FEDERAL COMMUNICATIONS COMMISSION OR OTHER APPROPRIATE AGENCY. IN ADDITION, CBS POLICY FORBIDS DISCRIMINATION BASED ON SEXUAL ORIENTATION.

NOTE: WHERE AN ASTERISK (*) APPEARS, THE QUESTION NEED BE ANSWERED ONLY IF YOU ARE OFFERED A POSITION.

PLEASE PRINT ALL INFORMATION

PERSONAL

Last Name	First	Initial	Today's date	Social Security number

Maiden Name*

Present address (Street, city, state, zip code) — Area code/Home telephone

Permanent address if different from above (Street, city, state, zip code)

Age*	Birth Date*	Are you a U. S. citizen? ☐ Yes ☐ No	Type visa		Shift Preferred

Do you have friends or relatives employed by CBS? Friends ☐ Yes ☐ No Relatives ☐ Yes ☐ No

Have you previously applied at CBS? ☐ No ☐ Yes When?

If yes, give name and relationship

Were you ever employed by CBS? ☐ No ☐ Yes From To

Have you been convicted of any law violation other than a minor traffic violation within the last 5 years? ☐ Yes ☐ No | Date | Place | Charge

Are you presently in good health? ☐ Yes ☐ No If "No", explain.

Applicant must pass a complete CBS physical examination as a condition of employment.

EMPLOYMENT

Business telephone number and extension where you can be reached | Position applied for | Salary desired $ | Date you could start

From Mo. Yr.	To Mo. Yr.	Previous employers (most recent first) Name / Address	Name of supervisor & title	Your position	Salary Beginning	Last	Reason for leaving

EDUCATION

From Mo. Yr.	To Mo. Yr.	Name and address of school	Type course or major	Graduate?	Degree	Year awarded
		Grammar				
		High or prep 1.				
		2.				
		Business or special				
		College 1.				
		2.				
		Graduate school				

U.S. MILITARY

From Mo. Yr.	To Mo. Yr.	Branch of service (If none, write "none")	Highest rank held	Date of discharge

106

Please complete reverse side

SPECIAL SKILLS

Business machines you can operate

Typing speed _____ Words per minute
☐ Electric
☐ Manual

Steno speed _____ Words per minute _____

Foreign languages (check only if fluent)

French	German	Italian	Spanish	Other
☐ Speak	☐ Speak	☐ Speak	☐ Speak	☐ Speak
☐ Read	☐ Read	☐ Read	☐ Read	☐ Read
☐ Write	☐ Write	☐ Write	☐ Write	☐ Write

CURRENT LICENSES

Radio Telephone (Class) ☐ 1st ☐ 2nd ☐ 3rd | City/State Issued

Ham Operator

Chauffeur (Classification)

Nurse (Type)

Projectionist

Professional Engineer | City/State Issued

Air Conditioning Engineer

Certified Public Accounting

Other

Other

HONORS ETC.

Honors, awards, publications, and technical societies

Type or name	Where	Date

Training and development programs

Type	Taken at	Date

HOBBIES OR SPECIAL INTERESTS (Comments Optional)

COMMENTS (OPTIONAL)

By applicant

REFERRALS

Referred to CBS by (indicate name)

Agency ☐ Fee ☐ No Fee	Newspaper Ad	Return From
		☐ Leave of Absence ☐ Maternity
College Recruiting	School ☐ Fee ☐ No Fee	CBS Employee Referral
Outside Referral	On my own	Other (Please explain)

Notify in emergency*

Name | Relationship

Address | Phone

I certify that the above information is correct and complete to the best of my knowledge and I understand that my permanent employment is dependent upon passing a physical exam and satisfactory check of my Personnel Record.

Signature

TO BE COMPLETED ONLY BY INTERVIEWER

COMMENTS

Initial interview by
☐ Personnel

(Name of Department)
☐ Other

107

APPLICATION FOR
HEALTH PLAN BENEFITS

PART I — TO BE COMPLETED BY EMPLOYEE

1. NAME OF EMPLOYER

2. GROUP POLICY NUMBER

3. CLAIM NUMBER   A. Have you previously submitted a claim for any member of your family? ☐ Yes ☐ No | B. If yes, give the Family Claim Number. If more than one, give highest number.   ☐ Unknown

4. EMPLOYEE
   A. Name (First, Initial, Last)
   B. Street Address
   C. City, State Zip Code
   D. Social Security Number

5. ON ALL CLAIMS, COMPLETE THIS SECTION
   A. Are You Married? ☐ Yes ☐ No   If Yes, complete the following
   B. Spouse's Name
   C. Is your spouse currently employed, or was your spouse employed in the past 12 months   ☐ Yes ☐ No
   D. If 5C is Yes, give Spouse's Current or Last Employer's

   Name

   Address

6. CLAIM INFORMATION
   A. Description of Illness or Injury

   B. First Date of Treatment   19

   C. Was the patient disabled and unable to work? ☐ Yes ☐ No
      If Yes, from   to   19

   D. Was the claim due to an accident? ☐ Yes ☐ No
      If Yes, give the date and time   19

   E. Was it a result of an automobile accident? ☐ Yes ☐ No

   F. A result of an occupational accident or illness? ☐ Yes ☐ No

7. PATIENT INFORMATION
   A. The claim is on   ☐ Myself   ☐ My Spouse   ☐ My Child
   B. Patient's Name   ☐ Male ☐ Female
   C. Patient's Date of Birth   19

8. ON CHILDREN'S CLAIMS, COMPLETE THE FOLLOWING
	Yes	No
A. Is the Child Married?	☐	☐
B. A Full-Time Student?	☐	☐
C. Full-Time Employed?	☐	☐
   D. If 8B or 8C is Yes, give School or Employer's

   Name

   Address

9. OTHER INSURANCE
   A. Do you, your spouse or your child have any other medical insurance ☐ Yes ☐ No   If Yes, complete the following
   B. Other Insurer's

   Name

   Address

   C. The Other Insurance is on a ☐ Group ☐ Individual basis
   D. If the other insurance is on a group basis, give the name and address of the other group (employer, union, school or organization) through whom the coverage is arranged.
      Other Group's

   Name

   Address

The above statements and answers, and any accompanying bills and statements are true and complete to the best of my knowledge and belief.
I authorize the release to and the use by THE COLONIAL LIFE INSURANCE COMPANY of any medical or other information needed in processing claim. A photocopy of this authorization shall be valid as the original.

► Signed (Employee, All Claims)   Date   ► Signed (Spouse, if Patient)   Date

PART II — TO BE COMPLETED BY EMPLOYER

10. Employee's Date of Employment   19 | 11. Job Title or Occupation | 12. Effective Date of Patient's Insurance   19

13. Has employment terminated? ☐ Yes ☐ No   If Yes, complete items 14 and 15 | 14. Date Last Worked   19 | 15. Reason for termination   ☐ Dismissed ☐ Quit ☐ Leave of Absence ☐ Disabled ☐ Lay-Off ☐ Retired

EMPLOYER'S NAME _____   TELEPHONE NO. _____

SIGNED BY_____ TITLE_____ DATE_____ 19___

108

NOTE: IF ALL QUESTIONS ARE NOT ANSWERED, THERE MAY BE A DELAY IN PROCESSING THIS CLAIM, AND THIS FORM MAY HAVE TO BE RETURNED TO YOU FOR COMPLETION.

GROUP HEALTH
INSURANCE CLAIM

PATIENT INFORMATION - TO BE COMPLETED BY EMPLOYEE

10. PATIENT'S NAME (First name, middle initial, last name)

11. PATIENT'S DATE OF BIRTH

12. PATIENT'S OR AUTHORIZED PERSON'S SIGNATURE
I Authorize the Release of any Medical Information Necessary to Process this claim.

13. I Authorize Payment of Medical Benefits to Undersigned Physician or Supplier for Service Described Below

SIGNED   DATE

SIGNED (Employee or Authorized Person)

PHYSICIAN OR SUPPLIER INFORMATION

14. DATE OF:	ILLNESS (FIRST SYMPTOM) OR INJURY (ACCIDENT) OR PREGNANCY (LMP)	15. DATE FIRST CONSULTED YOU FOR THIS CONDITION	16. HAS PATIENT EVER HAD SAME OR SIMILAR SYMPTOMS?

YES   NO

17. DATE PATIENT ABLE TO RETURN TO WORK

18. DATES OF TOTAL DISABILITY
FROM   THROUGH

DATES OF PARTIAL DISABILITY
FROM   THROUGH

19. NAME OF REFERRING PHYSICIAN

20. FOR SERVICES RELATED TO HOSPITALIZATION GIVE HOSPITALIZATION DATES
ADMITTED   DISCHARGED

21. NAME & ADDRESS OF FACILITY WHERE SERVICES RENDERED (If other than home or office)

22. WAS LABORATORY WORK PERFORMED OUTSIDE YOUR OFFICE?
YES   NO   CHARGES:

23. DIAGNOSIS OR NATURE OF ILLNESS OR INJURY, RELATE DIAGNOSIS TO PROCEDURE IN COLUMN D BY REFERENCE TO NUMBERS 1, 2, 3, ETC. OR DX CODE

1.

2.

3.

4.

24. A DATE OF SERVICE	B* PLACE OF SERV-ICE	C FULLY DESCRIBE PROCEDURES, MEDICAL SERVICES OR SUPPLIES FURNISHED FOR EACH DATE GIVEN	D DIAGNOSIS CODE	E CHARGES	F COMMENTS
		PROCEDURE CODE (IDENTIFY:) (EXPLAIN UNUSUAL SERVICES OR CIRCUMSTANCES)			

25. SIGNATURE OF PHYSICIAN OR SUPPLIER

26.

27. TOTAL CHARGE   28. AMOUNT PAID   29. BALANCE DUE

31. PHYSICIAN'S OR SUPPLIER'S NAME, ADDRESS, ZIP CODE & TELEPHONE NO.

SIGNED   DATE

30. YOUR SOCIAL SECURITY NO.

32. YOUR PATIENT'S ACCOUNT NO.

OR

33. YOUR EMPLOYER I.D. NO.

*PLACE OF SERVICE CODES

1 — (IH) — INPATIENT HOSPITAL
2 — (OH) — OUTPATIENT HOSPITAL
3 — (O) — DOCTOR'S OFFICE

4 — (H) — PATIENT'S HOME
5 —   DAY CARE FACILITY (PSY)
6 —   NIGHT CARE FACILITY (PSY)

7 — (NH) — NURSING HOME
8 — (SNF) — SKILLED NURSING FACILITY
9 —   AMBULANCE

O — (OL) — OTHER LOCATIONS
A — (IL) — INDEPENDENT LABORATORY
B —   OTHER MEDICAL/SURGICAL FACILITY

APPLICATION
FOR JUNIOR COLLEGE

GRAND RAPIDS JUNIOR COLLEGE — DATA FORM

→ SEE PAGE OPPOSITE FOR CODES

STUDENT'S SOCIAL SECURITY NUMBER
☐☐☐ — ☐☐ — ☐☐☐☐

(A) RESIDENCE CODE	(B) COUNTY CODE	(C) MS	(D) PEB	(E) SEX	BIRTHDATE

BIRTHDATE: MONTH · DAY · YR.

This form **MUST** be filled out in order for you to be accepted.

DIRECTIONS:
The Student Data Form is designed to be used to generate the initial college date processing record for each student. The accurate completion of this form is very important to insure accuracy of the student's record.

INSTRUCTIONS
Print within squares only using capital letters. Use only the number of squares allotted, abbreviating if necessary.

LAST NAME

FIRST NAME

MIDDLE INIT.

MAIDEN NAME

HOME ADDRESS

NUMBER	STREET NAME	DIRECTION

CITY	STATE	ZIP CODE	TELEPHONE AREA CODE	NUMBER

MAILING ADDRESS (FILL IN IF DIFFERENT FROM HOME ADDRESS)

NUMBER	STREET NAME	DIRECTION

CITY	ZIP CODE	TELEPHONE NUMBER	(H) FLD.	(J) ET.	(K) CL.

PLACEMENT

(L) PLACEMENT CURRICULUM CODE	(P) HIGH SCHOOL YEAR GRAD.	HIGH SCH. CODE	(M) NEXT COLLEGE CODE	CHECK IF YOU ARE A VET.

To qualify for resident tuition (indicated by #1 in space 12, column 1) you must have lived within the Grand Rapids School District for at least six (6) consecutive months prior to beginning of the semester for which you wish to enroll.

I certify that the information on this sheet is true and correct, and realize that giving misinformation subjects me to immediate dismissal from Grand Rapids Junior College.

WILL YOU NEED ASSISTANCE
IN JOB PLACEMENT UPON GRADUATION? ☐ YES ☐ NO

WILL YOU NEED ASSISTANCE
IN EXPLORING A CAREER CHOICE? ☐ YES ☐ NO

_____
STUDENT'S SIGNATURE

110

CODE SHEET

A – RESIDENCY (CODE)

1 - Resident of the School District of Grand Rapids
2 - Resident of Michigan but not Grand Rapids Sch. Dist.
3 - Out of State Resident

B – COUNTY RESIDENCE

(where you now live)

03 Allegan
08 Barry
34 Ionia
41 Kent
59 Montcalm
61 Muskegon
62 Newago
70 Ottawa
00 Other Michigan County
84 Outside State of Michigan

C – MARITAL STATUS (MS)

M Married
S Single
D Divorced
W Widowed
L Legally Separated

D – PREDOMINANT ETHNIC BACKGROUND (PEB)

F - Foreign Student (Non-permanent resident)
I - American Indian or Alaskan Native
N - American Black, American Negro, Afro-American
O - Asian or Pacific Islander
S - Hispanic
W - White; Non-Hispanic origin

E – SEX

M - Male
F - Female

F – STATES

AK   Alaska
AL   Alabama
AZ   Arizona
AR   Arkansas
CA   California
CZ   Canal Zone
CO   Colorado
CT   Connecticut
DE   Delaware
DC   District of Columbia
FL   Florida
GA   Georgia
GU   Guam
HI   Hawaii
ID   Idaho
IL   Illinois
IN   Indiana
IA   Iowa
KS   Kansas
KY   Kentucky
LA   Louisiana
ME   Maine
MD   Maryland
MA   Massachusetts
MI   Michigan
MN   Minnesota
MS   Mississippi
MO   Missouri
MT   Montana
NB   Nebraska
NV   Nevada
NH   New Hampshire
NJ   New Jersey
NM   New Mexico
NY   New York
NC   North Carolina
ND   North Dakota
OH   Ohio
OK   Oklahoma
OR   Oregon
PA   Pennsylvania
PR   Puerto Rico
RI   Rhode Island
SC   South Carolina
SD   South Dakota
TN   Tennessee
TX   Texas
UT   Utah
VT   Vermont
VA   Virginia
VI   Virgin Islands
WA   Washington
WV   West Virginia
WI   Wisconsin
WY   Wyoming

H – PLACEMENT FIELD (FLD)

L - Liberal Arts and Science
B - Business and Technology (includes Health)
D - Developmental
S - Special

J – ENROLLMENT TYPE (ET)

N - New Student
T - Transfer Student (from another college to J.C.)
R - Returning from last Semester
O - Returning from other than last Semester
G - Guest

K – CLASS LEVEL (CL)

F - Freshman
S - Sophomore
P - Post Graduate

M – NEXT COLLEGE

01 Alma
02 Aquinas
03 Calvin
04 Central Mich. Univ.
05 Eastern Mich. Univ.
06 Ferris State College
07 Grand Valley State
08 G.R. Baptist Bible Col.
09 Hope
10 Kalamazoo College
11 Mich. Tech. Univ.
12 Mich. State Univ.
13 Olivet College
14 Univ. of Mich.
15 Univ. of Mich.-Dearborn
16 Wayne State Univ.
17 Western Mich. Univ.
18 Other

P – HIGH SCHOOLS

GRAND RAPIDS

010 Catholic Central
001 Central
068 City School
002 Creston
009 Gr. Rapids Christian
006 Marywood
007 Mt. Mercy
003 Ottawa Hills
004 South
061 Street Academy
005 Union
062 Walbridge
011 W. Catholic
060 Gr. Rapids Adult H.S.

OTHER MICHIGAN

012 Allegan

063 Allendale
064 Baptist Academy
013 Belding
014 Byron Center
015 Caledonia
016 Calvin Christian
017 Cedar Springs
018 Comstock Park
019 Coopersville
058 Covenant Christian
020 E. Grand Rapids
066 Forest Hills Central
067 Forest Hills Northern
022 Fremont
069 Fruitport
023 Godwin
024 Grand Haven
025 Grandville
026 Grant
027 Greenville
070 Hamilton
028 Holland
029 Holland Christian
030 Hopkins
031 Howard City
032 Hudsonville
033 Ionia
059 Jenison
034 Kelloggsville
035 Kenowa
036 Kent City
037 Kentwood
071 Lakewood
038 Lee
039 Lowell
040 Newaygo
041 Northview
043 Ravenna
044 Reed City
045 Rockford
046 Rogers
047 Saranac
048 South Christian
049 Sparta
050 Spring Lake
051 Thornapple-Kellogg
072 Tri-County
052 Unity Christian
053 Wayland
054 West Ottawa
055 White Cloud
056 Wyoming
057 Zeeland
097 Other Michigan H.S.
098 Out of State H.S.
099 Foreign H.S.

CURRICULUM CODES

OCCUPATIONAL CURRICULUMS

128 Accounting, Associate
912 Air Cond., Refrig., & Heating, Associate
924 Air Cond., Refrig., & Heating, Certificate
951 Apprenticeship
925 Architectural Drafting, Associate
929 Architectural Drafting, Certificate
301 Associate Degree Nursing
921 Automotive Certificate
922 Automotive Technology, Associate
102 Business Administration, Associate
120 Child Development, Associate
114 Clerical Certificate
104 Clerical Receptionist, Associate
934 Construction Technology, Associate
808 Criminal Justice, Associate
105 Data Processing, Associate
115 Data Processing, Certificate
906 Electronics, Associate
121 Fashion Merchandising, Associate
914 Fire Science Technology, Associate
123 Food Service Certificate
124 Hotel, Motel Management, Associate
122 Interior Design/Furnishings, Associate
920 Machine Tool Certificate
127 Management & Superv., Associate

125 Marketing, Associate
116 Marketing, Certificate
904 Mechanical Drafting, Associate
928 Mechanical Drafting, Certificate
908 Industrial Technology, Associate
933 Photography Technology, Associate
126 Property & Casualty Insurance, Associate
926 Radio & TV Repair, Certificate
112 Secretarial, Executive, Associate
117 Secretarial, Certificate
119 Secretarial, Legal, Associate
118 Secretarial, Medical, Associate
931 Welding, Certificate
932 Welding, Associate

LIBERAL ARTS AND TRANSFER CURRICULUMS

901 Architecture
201 Art
501 Biology
101 Business Admin.
701 Chemistry
520 Crop and Soil Science
502 Dental Hygiene
106 Distributive Educ.
802 Economics
702 Engineering
910 Engineering Tech.
401 English
519 Environmental Science
202 Foreign Language
503 Forestry

710 Geology (Earth Science)
805 History
504 Home Economics
909 Industrial Arts
911 Industrial Engineering
402 Journalism
006 Liberal Arts (general)
506 Liberal Arts (biology)
703 Liberal Arts (physics)
806 Liberal Arts (social science)
403 Library Science
704 Mathematics
507 Medical Technology
509 Mortuary Science
203 Music
510 Natural Resources
511 Nursing
513 Occupational Therapy
711 Oceanography
521 Optometry
512 Pharmacy
602 Physical Education
514 Physical Therapy
705 Physics
807 Criminal Justice (police admin.)
810 Political Science
515 Pre-Dental
811 Pre-Law
516 Pre-Medical
812 Psychology
111 Secretarial
813 Social Work
814 Sociology
404 Speech
518 Veterinary Science
799 WMU Engr. Tech.

TEACHING

801 Teaching, Coop. Intern, CMU
804 Teaching, Elementary

803 Teaching, Elem. Intern MSU
601 Teaching, Elem. Phys. Ed.
204 Teaching, Sec. Art
517 Teaching, Sec. Biology
113 Teaching, Sec. Business
706 Teaching, Sec. Chemistry
405 Teaching, Sec. English
205 Teaching, Sec. Foreign Language
917 Teaching, Sec. Industrial Arts
406 Teaching, Sec. Journalism
708 Teaching, Sec. Mathematics
206 Teaching, Sec. Music
603 Teaching, Sec. Phys. Ed.
709 Teaching, Sec. Physics
407 Teaching, Sec. Speech

HEALTH CURRICULUMS

302 Dental Assisting, Associate
301 Associate Degree Nursing
304 Dental Hygiene, Associate
306 Dental Lab Tech, Associate
307 Respiratory Therapy, Certificate
303 Practical Nursing
305 Radiological Technician (X-Ray) Associate

SPECIAL CURRICULUM CODES

007 Undecided Curriculum — Transfer
008 Undecided Curriculum — Occupational
003 Early College Enrollment
005 Grace Bible College
001 Blodgett Hospital Nursing
002 Butterworth Hospital Nursing

111

CAR REGISTRATION FORM

APPLICATION FOR CERTIFICATE OF TITLE — COMMONWEALTH OF VIRGINIA — DIVISION OF MOTOR VEHICLES

OWNER INFORMATION

OWNER'S NAME (FIRST, MIDDLE, LAST) | **SOCIAL SECURITY OR EMPLOYER ID. NO.**

CO-OWNER'S NAME (FIRST, MIDDLE, LAST) | **SOCIAL SECURITY OR EMPLOYER ID. NO.**

CITY/COUNTY OF RESIDENCE | **GARAGED IN CITY/COUNTY OF** | Social Security Number (if any) is mandatory by Section 46.1-52 of the Code of Virginia (1950) as amended. Used for record keeping purposes.

OWNER'S ADDRESS | **CITY** | **STATE** | **ZIP**

LIEN INFORMATION

THE MOTOR VEHICLE DESCRIBED HEREIN IS FREE AND CLEAR OF ANY LIENS EXCEPT AS NOTED BELOW. IF NO LIENS, INDICATE "NONE."

FIRST LIEN | **AMOUNT OF LIEN** | **TYPE OF LIEN (SEE BELOW)** | **DATE OF LIEN**

LIENOR'S NAME

ADDRESS | **CITY** | **STATE** | **ZIP**

SECOND LIEN | **AMOUNT OF LIEN** | **TYPE OF LIEN (SEE BELOW)** | **DATE OF LIEN**

LIENOR'S NAME

ADDRESS | **CITY** | **STATE** | **ZIP**

TYPES OF LIENS

S/A - Security Agreement	C/M - Chattel Mortgage	R/T - Reserve Title	Tax Lien
C/S - Conditional Sales	D/T - Deed of Trust	L/A - Lease Agreement	E/T - Equipment Trust

SOURCE OF OWNERSHIP

CHECK ONE: ☐ NEW ☐ USED | **DATE OF PURCHASE** | **SALE PRICE (NO DEDUCTION FOR TRADE-IN)** | **2% SALES AND USE TAX**

FROM WHOM PURCHASED | **VIRGINIA DEALER LICENSE NO.**

ADDRESS | **CITY** | **STATE** | **ZIP**

WAS MOTOR VEHICLE PREVIOUSLY REGISTERED OR TITLED IN VIRGINIA (CHECK ONE) ☐ YES ☐ NO

VEHICLE INFORMATION

YEAR | **MAKE** | **BODY STYLE** | **ID. NO.** | **ODOMETER READING (AT TIME OF TRANSFER)** | **SHIPPING WEIGHT** LBS.

FOR TRUCKS, TRACTORS AND TRAILERS ONLY | **EMPTY WEIGHT** LBS. | **GROSS WEIGHT** LBS. | **GROSS WEIGHT COMBINATION** LBS. | **NO. OF AXLES**

BODY STYLE (CHECK ONE)

2 DR { ☐ SDN ☐ HT ☐ SW }
4 DR { ☐ SDN ☐ HT ☐ SW }
Truck { ☐ Pickup ☐ Panel ☐ Tractor ☐ Other }
Trailer { ☐ Utility/Boat ☐ House ☐ Semi ☐ Other }
☐ Bus (Seating Capacity ____)
☐ Motorcycle
☐ Other _____ (Specify)

IS THIS VEHICLE WITHIN ALL LEGAL LICENSABLE DIMENSIONS AND AXLE WEIGHTS (40 FEET IN LENGTH - 8 FEET IN WIDTH - 13 1/2 FEET IN HEIGHT)? ☐ YES ☐ NO

NON-RESIDENTS POWER OF ATTORNEY ONLY APPLYING TO NON-RESIDENTS AND CORPORATIONS NOT DOMESTICATED IN VIRGINIA

That I/we acting under and pursuant to the provisions of Chapter 541 of the Acts of 1958, General Assembly of Virginia, as now or hereafter amended, have made, constituted and appointed and under these presents do make, constitute and appoint the Commissioner of the Division of Motor Vehicles of the Commonwealth of Virginia, and his successor or successors in office, to be my/our true, and lawful agent and attorney-in-fact upon whom all legal processes against and notices to me/us may be served in any action or legal proceedings brought as the result of the operation and/or use of all motor vehicles titled or licensed in my/our name in the State of Virginia, and he is hereby authorized to enter an appearance in my/our behalf in any case or proceedings; and I/we hereby stipulate and agree that any lawful process against or notice to me/us which is duly served on said agent and attorney-in-fact shall be of the same legal force and validity as if served on me/us.

I/We hereby make application for a Certificate of Title for the vehicle described herein and for that purpose certify that the above facts are true and valid. All owners must sign.

Signature of Owner _____ Date _____

Signature of Co-Owner _____ Date _____

FOR DMV USE ONLY

SALES PRICE	$_____
2% TAX	$_____
TITLE FEE	$ 7.00
LICENSE FEE	$_____
UMV FEE	$_____
TRANSFER FEE	$_____
TOTAL	$_____

112